Worshiping Disorders

Calling Out Irreverent and Uncivil Attitudes in Christian Worship

Rev. (Dr.) Samuel E. Nweze

Copyright © 2021 Samuel E. Nweze

All rights reserved. No part of this publication may be reproduced, distributed, or transmitted in any form or by any means, including photocopying, recording, or any other electronic or mechanical methods, without the prior written permission of the publisher, except in the case of brief quotations embodied in critical reviews and certain other noncommercial uses permitted by copyright law. For permission, write to the publisher at:

Greatness University Publishers
London, UK
www.greatnessuniversity.co.uk

ISBN: 978-1-913164-36-2
ISBN-13: 978-1-913164-36-2

DEDICATION

This book is dedicated to my mother Rhoda, who prayed me into faith in Christ; to my father Erastus who helped nurture that faith to maturity and to all the Christians who are committed to a reverential worship of the Almighty God, as well as show civility to fellow worshipers.

Worshiping Disorders

CONTENTS

Acknowledgments	7
Preface	9
Foreword	13
Worship in the Line of Fire	17
A Culture of Disrespect	27
Historical Background	37
Perspectives and Postures in Worship	53
The Problem of Lateness	69
The Abuse of Mobile Gadgets/ Devices	95
Busy Bodies: Bedded Pews	111
"Dressing for Church"	137
Beer-Parlor Attitudes & Canal Indulgences	163
Waiting it Out	181
Conclusion	195
Going Forward	199
References	203
Endorsements	209
About the Author	213

ACKNOWLEDGMENTS

I am very glad that finally, this book has become a reality. However, this wouldn't have happened without the contributions of a number of people who deserve some mention.

First, I give all glory to God without whose inspiration this book would never have been conceived in the first place. Thank you, Jesus!

Next of course is my beloved wife, Mrs Ebere Nnenna Nweze (PhD), who also doubles as the "Editor-in-the House". Apart from pushing me real hard all the time, she very painstakingly proof-read and corrected the entire manuscript, injecting very valuable ideas as she went along. O how I love you my "FL"!

To Professor Paul Henry De Neui, who from my days at North Park Theological Seminary Chicago encouraged me to write I say, thank you! This book is the first fruit of your encouragement but will surely not be last.

I will not forget my friends Reverends Doug and Jodi Fondell, Pastors at the American Church in Paris, France. You both made concerted efforts to help me kick-start my pastoral education. Your efforts paid off in a big way. Besides, your humble dispositions and hard work remained a true source of inspiration to me long after we parted ways. Thank you!

To my dear friend Bishop Ransom Stephen of Our Father's House Intl. (New Life Gospel Centre), Yola, Adamawa State Nigeria I say 'mma mma'! The Lord is using you tremendously.

To members of my church in Hallunda, Sweden, you have been such a joy to me. Thank you for letting me shepherd you, even in all my imperfections. May the Lord bless you real good!

Finally, to my four wonderful children, Kenny, Daniel, Lily and Onyinyechi, I love you very church.

PREFACE

Sandwiched between what Frederick Lewis Donaldson called "The Seven Social Sins" in a sermon which he delivered at Westminster Abbey, London, on March 20, 1925 is something he called "Worship without Sacrifice." Among the social sins that Donaldson mentions are: 'Wealth without work' 'Pleasure without conscience'; 'Knowledge without character'; 'Commerce without morality'; 'Science without humanity'; and 'Politics without principle'. For worship to be characterised with these vices as 'a social sin' is to say the least, a very huge and embarrassing indictment. God expects Christians to understand their very calling and the demands of the Scriptures concerning worship but often many Christians fall short. This book will tell you that worship demands great sacrifice. It will also tell you that worship demands character. In addition, you will learn that the call for civility is of the essence in worship where civility is a biblical call to treat others the way you want to be treated. Of a truth, worship must begin with character in order for it to be meaningful. If worship lacks character and discipline, it becomes merely some piece of theatrical performance packaged and delivered to another god, not the God that Christians worship. I invite Christians who want to discover the 'little foxes that spoil the vine of orderly worship' to follow me on a trip through this book.

Worshiping Disorders

When I visit different churches and attend many Christian events that provide opportunities to offer worship to God, I often realize a recurring pattern. These are patterns of undesirable conducts that may undermine everything the people have always wanted to do at such gathering which is simply to worship God. In *Worshiping Disorders,* I have attempted to identify and expose some of these patterns. I do not claim that these things are previously unknown to many who will read this book. However, they are things that many may not take seriously yet they can be destructive agents against meaningful worship experiences. What else can negate claims to true worship than when a worshiper begins to manifest disrespectful behaviors towards the worshiped and uncivil attitudes towards fellow worshipers capable of infringing on their rights to enjoying undisturbed experience? These patterns and behaviors often negate some Christians' claims to be true worshipers.

One might wonder if this author has the pedigree to comment on such a touchy topic as this. From two perspectives, I feel that I stand in a privileged position to comment on a subject of this magnitude. First, as a long-time worship leader who has exercised my gifts and calling across a number of continents, I have over time, observed unseemly behaviors and attitudes during the most intense moments of Christian worship services. Suffice it to say that some of the conducts both from up the altar and down to the pews have often left sour taste in my mouth. Second, I have sat on the pews of different categories of churches also across different continents and I have not been too proud of the ways and manners people behaved during church services and other Christian worship events. So, I have been both a culprit and a victim of uncivil behaviors in worship just like most of you who are reading this book have as well.

I have presented this book in two parts. Part one covers the general introduction of the book's title and addresses the factors that engender uncivil behaviors in worship; the unseen hands, kind of, that make worshipers behave the way they do without realizing what they are doing. Also in this section is a summary of both the Jewish and early Christian attitudes to worship. This section concludes with an examination of a few perspectives in worship and attempting to examine worship behaviors both from the Bible's point of view and from the point of view of traditional religion and other major religions.

Part two is an exposition of some attitudes and behaviors I refer to as practical disorders in worship. In this part, some of the major areas where a clear lack of reverence and civility towards both the worshiped and fellow worshipers are in full display are examined with some changes proffered. The few issues I point out are not exhaustive so I hope that reader would be able to identify their particular areas of weakness and repent from them.

The book concludes by offering some helpful suggestions aimed at helping every Christian to return to true and reverential worship to God. The book also suggests ways to treat fellow worshipers with civility so that everyone's right to worship in an atmosphere of tranquillity will be guaranteed. If any reader finds some points in the book too accusatory or judgemental, please understand that my overarching intention is to motivate us to review our behaviour in God's presence whenever we gather to worship; not to criticize or condemn.

Finally, I would like to advise that where we seem to have fallen short, we should humbly repent; where we seem to have acted in ignorance, I challenge us to become more knowledgeable. Most importantly, I hope that we all will ultimately come to a decision to renew our commitment to reverence God more and to bring orderliness and civility to the congregants in all our worship events.

Note: All Scriptural references are taken from the New International Version (NIV), except otherwise stated.

Samuel Enyeribe Nweze

FOREWORD

From the beginning of times God had demanded absolute reverence and obedience from the people he has created to worship him. In the Garden of Eden, Adam and Eve fell out of favor with God because of irreverent disobedience to a simple command. In the very first of the Ten Commandments given to Israel through Moses, God declared that he was a jealous God who wouldn't share the space of worship with any other god. Consequently, whenever the people of Israel turned away from him to other gods, or undermined reverence to him, he had momentarily abandoned them to their fate and some consequences following. However, in our days people seem to get away with such attitudes in both private and corporate worship activities often with the lame excuse that "we are in the dispensation of grace"

This raised a question; has God changed or has he lowered his expectations in our times? Or are we who are called to worship him today guilty of the same taking-for-granted attitude exhibited by our fore fathers in the Faith? No! God has not changed neither is he about to do so. Granted that we are in the dispensation of grace yet our irreverence should be called out for what it is – indiscipline and a lack of self control over our choices when we come into the presence on God.

God's desire and demand for respect and honor are

Worshiping Disorders

no less important in the present time as they were in times of old. Rather, it is us, God's people who live in this time that have sought to treat God the same casualness with which we treat other issues today. Invariably, many of us have been seduced by some modern day worldly philosophies and attitudes that seem to encourage us to promote self and comfort over and above every other thing including God. Moreover, life nowadays has moved to the fast lane! There is a rat race to get so much done at the shortest possible time especially with the introduction of myriad of technological gadgets and apps. So we also seem to wholeheartedly subscribe to a 'fast food' worship culture. Sadly, some worshipers are caught up in the web of a cacophony of distractions and disorderly attitudes that show great disrespect to God and other worshipers without remorse. Sadly too, there have been few voices of rebuke as these attitudes have become increasingly rationalized and accepted as markers of modernity.

So, I consider it a great privilege to read and edit a book that exposes the prevalent irreverent attitudes towards worship. In the book **Worshiping Disorders**, the author put in very clear perspectives, problems that most people have always spoken about in hushed tones. He very painstakingly highlights the different disorderly behaviors that characterize Christian worship these days and discusses some of the unseen causes of these attitudes. In highlighting these practices, the author doesn't presume to act as a judge of other believers. Rather, he invites all worshipers to a family conversation about how to treat both God and fellow worshipers. The author's intention in the book is not to present a manual of faults but to invite fellow members of the family of God to examine their attitudes with a view to holding fast that which is good while discarding that which does not give God glory and that which does not give other believers respect.

I suggest that Christians read this book prayerfully and with great sense of humility with which the author has written to both himself and his fellow brothers and sisters. I also encourage very Christian reading this book to look out for the particular ways in which he or she has knowingly and sometimes unknowingly shown irreverent attitudes and disorderly behaviors in both private and corporate worship. Identifying these behaviors should be the first step to repenting and turning away from those. It is noteworthy that the author also suggests some practical ways to overcome these acts of disorderliness. It will help greatly to pay heed to his recommendations.

All in all, God demands that those who worship him must do so in spirit and truth and part of this truth is to examine the attitudes towards him 'truthfully'. This is what I think the author has accomplished by writing this book. God expects and orderliness and civility in his house. I think the author by writing this book wishes to encourage the application of Civility in relationships between Christians. Finally, I must add that as much as this book has been written with the ordinary Christian worshiper in mind, its well-researched presentation also makes it a veritable resource material for researchers and Christian theologians. The problems identified cut across lands, different denominational cultures thereby also making it a book for the global Christian community.

I hope that all who read this book will allow its message to work out great order in their worship experience as well as lead them to the recovery of deep reverence for God who has lovingly called them to worship Him.

Ebere Nnenna Nweze (PhD)
Stockholm, Sweden
August, 2021

WORSHIP IN THE LINE OF FIRE

Christian worship is under intense enemy attack. Satan doesn't want God's people to worship and praise him as they ought to and as he rightly deserves. Consequently, Satan has been in the habit of playing the spoiler role at gatherings where Christians gather to worship the only true God. Satan does not like and has never liked that the redeemed worship God alone; he too wants to be worshiped! Satan's desire dates back to the time when he was a ministering angel in heaven. He saw himself as equal to God and paraded himself as such. Even when he was cast down to the earth, he did not give up. Ever since then Satan appeared to have vowed to ensure that God-worship will be corrupted. Thus he attacks everywhere and every place where people are determined to worship God in spirit and in truth. For example, he contended with God in the Garden of Eden by turning man away from God to focus on him instead. In this dispensation of grace too, Satan has not let off. Three times Satan prodded Jesus to worship him. But three times Jesus rebuked him and told him emphatically that worship belongs to God only.

Sadly, not many Christians seem aware at all that this most essential aspect of a Christian's duty has strangely come under intense attack. Consequently, Satan's plots appear to largely achieve the desired results. But to continue avoiding drawing more attention to this longstanding satanic assault is tantamount to continuing to allow him to succeed in this aspect of our Christian life where he seems to hurt us all the most and where God expects us to resist him like Jesus did. God's Word enjoins us to "Resist the devil and he will flee" from us, (James 4:7 NKJV). Satan's antics can be resisted. But to do so, God's people must first understand his modus operandi.

Several authors have written books and countless articles concerning Christian worship. However, few appear to have specifically addressed this aspect of Satan's continuing assault on worship. Most of what we see or read are mere general statements concerning worship in the church, much of which are couched in high-sounding theological language. But the peculiar and practical challenges that Christian worshipers face in our day require more of direct confrontation than mere intellectual theologizing. A popular African idiomatic expression says that "When a bird begins to fly without perching, the bird hunter also learns to shoot without stopping". Christian worship is in the line of fire. The issues run very deep and are mostly practical and human-made, but with a strong ideological interference that we all must identify and tackle with the strongest ferocity.

Few Christians if any seem to sometimes ask the obvious question, "Are we truly worshiping?" But this is precisely the question I will pose to all readers of this book, "Are we indeed truly worshiping?" I raise this question with the highest sense of humility, fully aware that God is the ultimate respondent to such a personal question because it is to him that all worship is directed. However, to the extent in which God himself has put watchmen and women over the gates of Jerusalem (Isaiah 62:6), a few of us must be willing and ready to identify when the thief sneaks in among God's folks with the intent to kill, to steal and to destroy, (John 10:10), which, are his three-fold agenda in the church - an agenda to which he remains faithfully and rigorously pursuant to. I will enjoin all who will read this book to follow me in this journey of humble exposition. I humbly invite you to forget about yourselves; your defensive instincts; your great wealth of knowledge and presuppositions; and your familiarity with God and submit to God's spirit as He helps us to identify the areas of disorders in our personal and corporate worship, lest we be found to be offering strange fire to The Most High God! I will now turn to a brief discussion of one of the ideological interferences that I consider a strong contributor to the careless attitude to worship being exhibited by many contemporary Christians.

The Changing Times

As I pointed out earlier, Christianity and Christian worship had already received the hard knocks before the arrival of the age of modern science and all its attendant philosophies and worldview. This was the time known as the age of Modernism. In the era of Modernism, science began to question the notion or dominance of religion as the only source of truth. This challenge posed a danger to all biblical claims of God as the creator of the universe, and thus of humanity. If science could prove absolutely that humanity came to be other than from God's creative activity as recorded in Genesis chapter one, then it would be futile to ascribe worship to such a God. Thankfully though, through a resolute faith and trust in the Scriptural provisions, the church struggled through this era and clung unto this God of creation, demonstrating this trust through continuously offering its resounding and unmitigated worship and praise fully to him. But a deadlier and subtler challenge was soon to emerge on the scene!

Postmodernism followed on the heels of Modernism. Postmodernism is the age mostly starting from the middle of the 20th Century AD up until the present when scientific knowledge combined with highly enhanced and sophisticated human reasoning to take on the steering wheel of the automobile of human existence. Once it became very comfortable on that steering wheel, it began to steer the direction of humanity away from God and towards its perceived purposes and directions. It is the age that says that reality is an individual construction. Put more simply, post-modernism can be defined as the age when every idea must be understood in relative terms and when individual reasoning determines what a person wants to believe in, be it religion, politics, social issues, ethics and morals as well as matters of sexuality and gender.

In his article, "What is Post modernism?" (2016) Jack Zevada cited Jim Leffel's statement that "Reality is in the mind of the beholder. Reality is what's real to me, and I construct my own reality in my mind."[1] This statement pretty much sums up the postmodern person's worldview.

Choices made by individuals on any one of such issues as are listed above namely, religion, ethics etc, are purely localized and individualistic and must not be announced in the public square. In a post modern mindset, there simply is no such thing as universally agreed principles, values and norms. It is a philosophy that says "I-do-it-because-I-like-it", or vice versa. This mindset completely repudiates any truths that anyone can possibly hold as absolute and this unfortunately; is the age in which the children of God must find the space and the audacity to worship him.

But you ask, what has a lecture on modernism and postmodernism got to do with a book on Christian worship? This quote by Steve Cornell (2006) will be helpful in addressing such a concern. In an online article Cornell refers to postmodern propositions as mere 'lies'. He defines the lies of postmodernism as "…the wholesale rejection of universal reason and absolute truth. It is the delusional mindset that there is no objective goodness and rightness. These

---
[1] Jack Zevada "What is Postmodernism?"

prevailing opinions have led to the dismissal of an absolute deity. Don't misunderstand; God is warmly welcomed in the postmodern world as long as he doesn't try to play God."[2]

This is precisely the point! By implication, the 'deity' to be dismissed as a result of these prevailing godless opinions is the creator-God, the God that Christians worship. Of a truth, the avowed purpose of a postmodern mindset is to significantly or completely diminish, perhaps even completely erase the image and personhood of the God of Israel and his value and significance to humans. Thus if you have a diminished sense of him then you will, if at all, worship him as a d-o-g instead of G-O-D. The point is that Christian worship has increasingly come under the threat of this type of dominant mindset. It is possible therefore that a person who subscribes to the prevalent post-modern mindset will have a sickly and questionable attitude to worship if they have one at all!

This is the assumption that resonates with the very thinking of this book, especially given the degree of observable changes in attitudes and character in the worship events of our day. Let us keep in mind that young people remain the most vulnerable to the post-modern appeal, and they are a significant group in the worship life of the church in the present and the future. The danger therefore, is far greater than we

---

[2]Steven W. Cornell, "What does postmodern mean?"

can imagine. Christian worship has been observably and effectively compromised in ways far too unimaginable. It is to highlight the manifestations of post-modern attitudes in Christian worship motivated me to write this book. These compromises and attitudes are what I refer to as *Worshiping Disorders.*

"Disorder" A Definition

The Webster's dictionary of modern English defines disorder as a" confusion or lack of order", a "breach of order or a disorderly conduct." Other synonyms for this word are: disarray, jumble, turbulence, mess up, disorganize, etc. From a medical point of view, disorder is defined is an anomaly-a disease of some sort. It is "a disturbance of function, structure, or both, resulting from a genetic or embryonic failure in development or from factors such as poison, trauma, or disease." (Medical dictionary). As a matter of fact, "disorder" is the name for everything that ought not to be; an aberration; a deviation from the desired norm. 'Disorder' largely describes every situation where absolute chaos reigns supreme. In fact, it refers to situations where things appear to have spiraled out of control.

Every word or expression above combines to aptly describe in some form everything that has gone wrong with the worship life of the Church of Jesus Christ in a postmodern era. As gloomy and pessimistic as that may sound to some readers, a good look at what goes on in many Christian fellowships and churches in our time would reveal that indeed a great disturbance, a turbulent storm of disorderliness and a breach of normal historical order of doing things as experienced by the worshipers of God in the historical past holds sway. Henry E. Horn (1972) laments this ugly development when he observes that "The line between what is done in church and what might be done at a demonstration on a social issue is erased. The sweep is irresistible. Few congregations can maintain their composure."[3] The sweep of disorderliness in many church's worship activities is indeed of indescribable proportions. Sometimes some worshipers might wonder whether they have ended up in the wrong place.

Simply put, there is a crisis of decorum and character in today's Christian worship due mainly to the prevailing influence of societal trends. The worship of God has never in history been reduced to sometimes mere theatrical shows or rowdy street disturbances as pointed out above, as evidenced in what goes on in many churches. Sometimes there is a sense that worship has been emptied of some things that the church has always considered as essential and intrinsic in its divine character. What goes on in our day is largely a distorted representation of some of the ways in which God was always worshiped from the beginning of creation. We are drifting away from everything that has always been regarded as normal

---

[3] Henry E. Horn, "Worship in Crisis", p.3

worship behavior.

Different environments do require different codes of conduct and behavior not least the church. As a matter of fact, the church, the presence of God more than any other place else deserves the noblest of conducts. But the things which collide with sensible conduct in worship are necessarily not the big theological questions that often form the discourse in theological circles. These are identifiable behavioral patterns that are very nauseating and annoying and at their worst stages of manifestation constitute insults to God himself. Indeed, they are things that the Scriptures would refer to as the "little foxes that spoil the vine" (Songs of Solomon 2:15).

These are the disorders that we are set to identify and attempt to address in order to educate ourselves on biblically and ethically acceptable ways of offering acceptable or reasonable sacrifice of worship to God. In all, the ultimate objective of this book would be to attempt to contribute to the restoration of order and etiquette to Christian worship by highlighting the ways Christians should NOT conduct themselves in worship. Anyone reading this book and who is guilty of one or more of these disorderly attitudes would feel inspired to prayerfully submit to the help of the Holy Spirit as well as take practical steps to correct them.

Worshiping Disorders

Worshiping Disorders

A CULTURE OF DISRESPECT

"Live as free people, but don't hide behind your freedom when you do evil." 1Pet.2:16[GWT]

Of all the religious faiths ever known to man, Christianity offers the highest levels of freedom to its adherents. No other religion comes even a distant second. Unfortunately, this freedom has been subject of abuse. Rather than embracing it as a just and laudable gesture from a loving God and worthy of appreciation and reciprocation, many Christians use this as 'liberty to sin'. Put in another way, God's civility towards his people often fails to attract its kind as a whole lot of uncivil behaviors are on open display in many gatherings purportedly dedicated to his worship. There are many examples to support this view.

The Bible does not impose for example, things like food codes, gender-based dress codes, or laws preferring one day over another on Christians. Similarly, the Bible offers no prescriptions for such other things as frequency and designated times for prayer, or the geographical direction a person must face during prayer. Also, the Bible does not impose special pilgrimages or religious seasons on Christians. Neither are Christians under any obligation of any kind to perform pre-prayer rituals such as washing of parts of the body; neither are they restricted to any special pattern of prayer or obligatory chants and recitations except such as are imposed by the tradition of particular Christian denominations. The Christian faith abhors all manner of coercion and Christian worshipers are scarcely under any form of strict patterns of behavior, something which every Christian understands full well.

On the contrary, it is a well-known fact that several major and minor religions are known to be very stringent about things such as these and many more. Some are particular about things as basic as food. For example, a Jew would give nothing in exchange for a *kosher* meal; neither would a Muslim strike any compromise to eat anything but *halal* meat. Most eastern religions characteristically insist on vegetarian or vegan diets as a matter of ritualistic compulsion. No Christian is known to be subjected to the above-mentioned religions-driven rituals. Also, no Christian feels threatened or compelled to desist from eating things such as pork or other types of meat or indeed any other thing considered abominable by many religions. Such legalistic observances and restrictions do not go hand in hand with the teachings of Jesus or the apostles. Where restrictions are imposed on people by any Christian group, such often comes as a result of not taking seriously or wrong interpretations of the teachings of the Bible on freedom in Christ. In the Bible, whenever circumstances came up that required unnecessary burdens or inconsequential restrictions to be placed on people, such were vehemently opposed.

For example, in chapter ten of Acts of the Apostles, Simon Peter received an angelic visitation three times, warning him that nothing created by God must be called unclean. This was said to a man that "became very hungry and wanted to eat" (Acts 10:10a). This is one of the texts often used by Christians to embrace every healthy creature of God as God's generous gift for human nourishment. So free is a Christian to eat every type of food that Paul the apostle, in 1 Corinthians chapter 8 absolves a person of any guilt for eating food sacrificed to idols. The only reason for abstinence from eating such food is based on Paul's warning in verse 9 of the same chapter. In this text Paul says, "Be careful, however, that the exercise of your rights does not become a stumbling block to the weak." (1Corinthians 8:9). In other words, a Christian operates with the knowledge that "for us there is but one God, the Father, from whom all things came and for whom we live; and there is but one Lord, Jesus Christ, through whom all things came and through whom we live.", (I Corinthians 8:6). That means that a Christian has a right to eat all things that are healthy. However, love for the wellbeing of the other rather than meaningless legalistic impositions is the reason for abstinence from eating such things. Such is the degree of the unparalleled freedom that Christians enjoy in the practice of their faith.

Let us consider yet another text that says something powerful concerning liberty in the Christian religion. This is a text which makes it clear that it is up to God to judge in matters of our choice of days and the food we eat; "Those who worship the Lord on a special day do it to honor him. Those who eat any kind of food do so to honor the Lord, since they give thanks to God before eating. And those who refuse to eat certain foods also want to please the Lord and give thanks to God." (Romans 14:6 NLT) Central in this text is the acknowledgment of God as the provider of all things. What is required here therefore is not to abhor this benevolence of God. Rather, what is required is that we receive it with thankfulness and gratitude. Once this is done, no one reserves the right to judge the one who embraces these gifts or legislate for that matter, on the extent of their enjoyment. This is exactly what all Bible-believing Christians who exercise themselves in the freedom in Christ have done in the practice of their faith throughout the history of the Christian faith. Those who have done otherwise are those who, out of their own volition preferred legalistic practice of the faith to the simplicity and freedom that the grace of God brought to humanity. But this freedom, just like every free gift, comes with great responsibility.

The High Cost of Liberty

Unbridled liberty in the hands of a people could have unspeakable negative consequences. There is a popular saying that "power corrupts, while absolute power corrupts absolutely". Whereas liberty, or freedom, isn't exactly the same as power, yet the same can be true of it. It would sound reasonable therefore

Worshiping Disorders

to conclude that freedom corrupts, while absolute freedom corrupts absolutely. Christians are not exempt from this tendency. As Apostle Paul warns, liberty in the hands of religious enthusiast can be abused (Galatians 5:13). When applied to our discussion on Christian worship, it is not hard to see that worship in the church appears to have been corrupted by the bi-products of God-given liberty as described in the preceding section. Christians appear to have lost the reverence and sacredness which once characterized Christian worship.

Much of the irreverent attitude exhibited by many worshipers towards God during worship can be attributed to two major reasons. First, God does not impose immediate punishment on Christian offenders for any misbehavior. Biblically, the reward for disobedience is a deferred promise, a promise of punishment for the unrepentant. Second, God's love and respect for his created beings would not permit him to turn them into robots that are remote-controlled from his throne. Consequently, he gave humans the ability to choose between reasonableness and its opposite; between civility and incivility; between good and evil; decorum, respect and good morals. As a matter of fact, God gave humans the choice between eternal punishment in hell and everlasting life in heaven. This is the reason it is often said that a person is a free moral agent graciously offered the unguarded freedom to choose. However, each individual is responsible for what he or she does with this freedom. So while some people see and treat

Worshiping Disorders

it as a rare gesture from a good God worthy of reciprocation through dedicated life of worship and reverence for him, others use it as a tool for selfish indulgences and life outside the giver.

As Pastor Ray Pritchard (2001) some Christians misinterpret, freedom even though godly freedom should be the desire of every true believer,

> "True freedom is the opportunity, ability, and the desire to do those things that will bring the deepest joy 10,000 years from now. Many things that people do in the name of "freedom" actually lead to their own destruction. That's why Christians should never envy the "freedom" of sinners. Often we look at people who sleep around and think, "That must be fun."[4]

Many people seem either aware or unaware of the destructive power of negative freedom, or they simply are unprepared to pay the inherent price often associated with freedom's positive aspect which is, to embrace it with great gratitude towards its giver and use much of it to his benefit and for the wellbeing of others. It appears that the church of Christ of the 21st Century has unfortunately been caught in the tangled web of the former. The misinterpretation and

---
[4] Ray Pritchard, "Risky Business: The other side of freedom"

misapplication of true godly freedom raises the question; does Christian worship practice in many Christians across different cultures still show contain utmost reverence to the utmost high, the one who chose to unbind rather than bind his followers? Attitudes and conducts at Christian worship events largely reflect patterns to the contrary. Much of what is witnessed is a clear lack of decorum and order that mirrors a world which has thrown all caution to the winds. Respect and reverence which once characterized society appears presently far-fetched. Even the once-held respect for the elderly appears in our day to be a thing of the past. Parents struggle to attract the commonest attention from their own children; something that was once taken for granted. In schools, teachers have gradually and painfully learned to lower their once non-negotiable expectation of respect and honor from students and pupils. Students and pupils now appear to make rather than follow the rules. In short, the popular injunction to "give honor to those to whom honor is due" (Romans 13:7) scarcely holds in our day. In the words of the famous poet John Keats re-echoed by Nigerian novelist Chinua Achebe, "things have indeed fallen apart"!

Having grown up in a non-Western world, one of my first encounters with culture shock during my early years of sojourn in Europe was to have children address me in ways that would be judged shockingly disrespectful, by the standards of the culture from which I moved to the continent. One of the hardest adjustments I had to make for example was to have to accept the fact that certain age-based cultural gestures were no longer things I could take for granted. The world facing me had become a "whatever" world, one in which there is an obvious leveling, where neither age nor status in life determined what to expect in terms of respect and social regard. The fact that laws in western societies forbid any application of pressure to get someone to behave in particular ways has not helped matters either. Such parental guidance which sometimes required a mild application of pressure on a child to comply with certain social and family values are clearly out of the question, thus giving disproportionate freedom to minors and adults alike to behave as they liked. What obtains instead in the country which I now call home is an "Om du vill" attitude, (Swedish expression for "If you so desire"). One then finds oneself living in an environment, albeit a very beautiful and enviable one for that matter, but one which boasts of every attraction of a postmodern mindset to the highest proportions.

Unfortunately, this type of philosophy in which everyone is supposed to know, choose and do what they desired, and at the times and occasions of one's own choosing has had, in my opinion, two very negative consequences on people's attitude towards the divine. First, people's ability to entrust themselves to the spiritual guidance of people positioned for such spiritual leadership is considerably weakened. Consequently, the previously unheard of egalitarian attitude in the practice of the Christian faith is on the increase, a sort of, do-it-yourself or a self-help mindset, completely alien to the Christian confession. The second consequence, which I already mentioned, forms the bedrock of this book is the spillover of a lack of respect for God. This aspect is no surprise especially when for example we consider what John the apostle wrote concerning love. He says, "Whoever claims to love God yet hates a brother or sister is a liar. For whoever does not love their brother and sister, whom they have seen, cannot love God, whom they have not seen." (1 John 4:20) Love for God is impossible without love for people because love in itself isn't just a learned behavior; it is God! God is love! In the same way when honor lacks a horizontal manifestation (honor toward fellow human beings); a vertical ascent (honor toward God) will be near impossible. A loss of respect for fellow humans is an obvious signature of a loss of respect for God who as the text says, we cannot see. This is precisely the worst danger that the church of Christ is facing in our day. There seems no more to be such things as sacrilegious acts in our time, so that a minister of the gospel risks receiving unapologetic verbal (and on occasion physical) beatings in the hands of just about anybody within the church. It appears as if the scriptural injunction to hold those who have rule over God's people especially those who teach the word of God in great honor has been deleted from the bible! (Hebrews 13:17). In this type of society, God can no longer be expected to be the super hero of very many people. Unfortunately, the one place where the consequences of all these negative patterns are obvious is the worship of the church. Conducts in most worship events shows a clear loss of the reverence that was once clearly evident among worshipers. As a matter of fact, the call to "Be still and know that I am God" (Psalm 46:10), appears to have been drowned by the deafening cacophony of this type of culture of disrespect in today's world. Whatever the case however, God remains God and his righteousness and generosity which moved him to offer freedom to the people he loves will not be altered.

HISTORICAL BACKGROUND TO CHRISTIAN WORSHIP

Christianity is a developmental religion. It just didn't happen; there's a history behind it. The genealogy of Jesus Christ can be traced back to a people; the Hebrews/Jews/Israelites – descendants of Abraham who God called out and multiplied. God gave these people specific instructions about how to practice worship that will be acceptable to him. He appointed priests and prophets of his own choosing and instructed them to lead his people in worshiping him. So we can look to the way this chosen people of God carried out worship practices for a few lessons on how God desires to be worshiped. Jesus himself inherited these practices and even declared that he didn't come to abolish them but to perfect them. His ministry transited from the practices of his Jewish parents to the new dispensation of grace. The apostles also bestrode these two dispensations so they carried aspects of the Jewish worship practices into the early church. In this chapter therefore, I will highlight both Jewish worship practices and the early church's worship practices.

Jewish Temple Worship

Jewish temple worship provides historical antecedents to how the God of the Christians should be worshiped. In all their stubbornness and disobedience, Israel remained constant and forthright in offering reverential and hearty worship to Yahweh. It must be understood that the Jewish nation was an experimental nation, a people belonging to God but who never really fully understood the magnitude of the privileged calling to be God's chosen people. Consequently, their story was constantly one of rising and falling; of obedience and disobedience; of loyalty and disloyalty. Each time they drifted into disobedience, their leaders would remind them of who they were, causing them to have a rethink and turn around.

However, while they had trouble with patient obedience to God's commands especially during those times when they became vulnerable in the hands of their many foes, they remained constantly aware of their calling as God's chosen people. This tenacious faith in God necessitated their deliverance from Egyptian slavery. As recorded in Exodus 7:16. God sent Moses to Pharaoh King of Egypt with the following unequivocal message, "The LORD, the God of the Hebrews, has sent me to say to you: Let my people go, so that they may worship me in the wilderness. But until now you have not listened." As we can see from that text, worship and sacrifice are the central reasons God called Israel out of Egypt. Consequently, irrespective of whatever weaknesses found in their lives, they never lost sight of this divine mandate. Whenever they strayed from this primary calling, they always found their way back in repentance.

Worshiping Disorders

In his book titled, *"Worship in Ancient Israel"* (1959), A.S, Herbert observed that Israel took worship very seriously. They understood worship as something much more than mere human act or words. To them, worship provided rare opportunities for them to rehearse and respond to God's disclosure of himself to them and his deliverance from Egyptian oppression in the most reverential ways. Hebrew worship was a purpose-driven activity, an act of whole-hearted obeisance given by a people to their creator and sustainer whom they constantly held in the highest esteem. They fully understood God's demands and expectations in this particular area. Thus whenever there was a negative change or shift in attitudes, or an inclination towards worshiping other gods or idols some of which they got exposed to throughout the time of their movements in the wilderness, God vehemently rebuked them through the prophets. In the more extreme violations they were put under God-sanctioned oppression by their enemies.

Israel also understood the peculiarity of their relationship with Yahweh such as the Covenant made between him and their father Abraham. As such, they were constantly aware of what was required of them in relation to Yahweh. This awareness made them tenaciously devoted to Yahweh and their worship of him was never to be a thing to trifle with. Herbert points out that, "It is this frame of reasoning, which determined the nature and direction" of Israel's worship[5]. In other words, God had so much significance for Israel that their consciousness was always filled by his presence among them. As Herbert further points out, they were so concerned about the ways and manners in which they worshiped God, fearing that he would depart from them if they did not worship him properly. Herbert points further to the role which significance or meaning played in Israel's taking their worship of Yahweh very seriously. They realized that they worshiped a God unlike any other god. This knowledge reflected in the ways in which they worshiped. Thus, Herbert uses a word such as "veneration" to describe the nature of Israel's worship. He observes that "No less important for an estimate of Israel's worship is the character of Him who is the object of veneration, for that in turn will affect the kind of worship that is offered to him."[6] What this means is that people's attitude to worship is a direct function of their understanding and experience of the object of their worship. Far too many Christians seem to have lost sense of who the God they worship really is and his place in their lives. Consequently, their veneration of him has become an unfortunate casualty.

H. H. Rowley (1967) makes a similar observation, pointing out the effect on Israel's worship of their realization of the kind of God they worshiped. The first point he identifies is 'adoration', observing that

---

[5] A.S. Herbert, "*Worship in Ancient Israel*" p. 5.
[6] Herbert p. 9

the Hebrews expressed this by their posture and not only by their words. The Hebrews, he observes "did not come with an easy familiarity into the presence of God, but were aware of his greatness and majesty, and came with a sense of privilege to his house."[7] This observation confirms that awareness greatly determines attitude. Awareness is the understanding of the limits and dangers of over familiarity. In a sense, and quite unfortunately too, there is this general feeling that Christian worshipers in our day have become all too familiar with God to the point that they seem to have lost every sense of his majesty and splendor. In relation to God, the Davidic call to "Serve the LORD with fear, and rejoice with trembling" (Psalm 2:11), appears to be largely falling on many deaf postmodern ears. Over-familiarity has brought such incapacity far too dangerous for everything the church is called upon to be with respect to their worship of God. The beginning of worship and praise lies in a person's willingness to accept God as supreme. When persons therefore, elevate themselves and their self-worth to levels where the former's supremacy is challenged in their minds, worship can no longer take place and such behavior accounts for some of the misconducts in the house of worship.

The second point that Rowley identifies is a crippling lack of 'awe and reverence' in Christian worship. He

---

[7] H.H. Rowley, "*Worship in Ancient Israel; Its Forms and Meaning*" p.257.

notes that the bible places no extra demand on Christian worshipers when they come to worship than simply to "recognize his glory and goodness."[8], pointing out that nothing can stand in the way of worship that begins with adoration and reverence. The biblical Jews worshiped God realizing the fact of their inadequacy; their desperate and constant need for God's grace and forgiveness. They never felt that they were doing God or the priests any favor by coming to worship, which is sometimes the case with some worshipers today. Marva J. Dawn (1995) has this to say concerning worship, "Our forebears perhaps took this reverence to an inordinate extreme in their austere rigidity or unwarranted terror, but now, sometimes the pendulum swings too far in the opposite direction, with the result that we turn Christ into merely a buddy and not the King of kings and Lord of lords."[9]

When people walk into church with a false sense of importance, they seem to forget that they owe their lives, gifts and possessions to the grace and mercy of God who they ignorantly treat like a 'buddy'. The fact is that such people show an ungrateful attitude. They fail to honor God. Some Christian worshipers tend to be very opportunistic. They want to experience God's power in their lives but are not prepared to honor him as God. The apostle Paul describes such people when he observed that "...For although they knew God,

---

[8] Rowley, p.259.
[9] Marva J. Dawn, "Reaching out without dumbing down" p.267.

they neither glorified him as God nor gave thanks to him…" (Romans 1:21a). One wonders why such people still claim the benevolences of this same God they so brazenly dishonor. God himself declares unequivocally, "…But I will honor those who honor me, and I will despise those who think lightly of me. (1Samuel 2:30) Author Dawn goes further to explain that the house of God "is a place for laughter and joyfulness, for tears of repentance or sadness, for silence and meditation, for the Word proclaimed. It is not a place for rudeness, noises that disrupt others, or irreverence for the special moments with God as is rampant in worship services today.[10]

It is therefore possible to assume that when Jesus drove the money changers and merchandisers away from the temple; all those who exhibited other forms of irreverent worshiping attitudes might have been among those who received the greatest weight of his chastisement. In the proverbial house of prayer of our present circumstances, Jesus would repudiate and chastise very many of what some Christians do and how they conduct themselves. The church is clearly not the place for careless fun and 'Vanity Fair' neither is the time of worship a time for self indulgence. Such was the case with Israel during one of the times that they lost focus of their calling to be a people of pleasure to God.

Moreover, the third commandment that God gave to

---

[10] Ibid

Israel through Moses was clear; "You shall not take the name of the Lord your God in vain, for the Lord will not hold him guiltless who takes his name in vain." (Exodus 20:7) This was a towering injunction to Israel, one which formed part of their covenant relationship with God. Israel, in all their stubbornness remained acutely aware of this charge to lift high the sacredness and integrity of Yahweh. This they had carefully sought to do all through the history of Jewish worship. Whenever there was a departure either in terms of the object or the manner or propriety of their worship, God frowned and sought to correct them in ways and manners that were sometimes very painful and consequential. For example, in Exodus chapter 32, Israel violated the first and second commandments and persuaded Aaron to make a golden calf for them to worship following Moses' delayed return from the mountain. God was fiercely so angry with them that he brought death upon them. God wanted to remain the beginning and the end of Israel's worship and would not allow for any intervening object among his people. Neither would God allow the camp of his people to be turned into a den of revelers and idolaters. This demand for focus and faithfulness in worship is as true today as it was in the days of ancient Israel.

The presence of the Ark of Covenant gave another window into the worship life of Israel. Although, just as many scholars rightly pointed out, Israel did not worship the Ark, yet the Ark significantly remained a symbol of their worship and a symbol of God's presence among them. Author Ángel Manuel Rodríguez articulated the essence of the Ark in the following words, "The Israelites did not worship the ark, but they sought the Lord there as the place where He would meet with them, and where they could offer Him their prayers and praises."[11] The Ark of Covenant was so revered in Israel that its presence was always accompanied by a cloud which symbolizes the glory and holiness of God. Wherever the Ark went, King David and all Israel followed it with great care and reverence, "celebrating with all their might before the LORD, with castanets, harps, lyres, timbrels, sistrums and cymbals." (2Samuel 6:5). God's presence as represented by the Ark was one which demanded absolute compliance to the stated rules and rituals. Any misconduct resulted in immediate fatality. For example, once when the cart conveying the Ark tripped, Uzzah reached out to save it and never lived to tell his story. This goes to show just how palpably and powerfully God's presence dwelt in the congregation of Israel and how seriously they regarded this presence and reflected that high regard in their daily lives and worship.

Indeed, Israel never had the luxury of treating worship with levity even though walking with God was a daily requirement of their lives. Looking at Israel who on occasion was grossly obstinate towards God no other people can be better example to teach the rest of us about the call to be worshipers of this

---

[11] A.M. Rodriguez, "The Ark of the Covenant"

God whose presence and influence remain among his people always. Therefore, we, the modern Christian worshipers have so much to learn from the chosen people of God.

Worship in the Early Church

The early Christians obviously struggled to keep their heads high after the ascension of Jesus to heaven. Their master, the one who was at the very centre of attention from the Roman and Jewish authorities was gone leaving them struggling to defend and advance a strange new religious movement in a purely Judeo-Roman region. Consequently, determining exactly what to do concerning the god-man who previously provided cover for them and who claimed divinity was no easy task whatsoever. For them and for many other followers of Jesus, the times were as confusing as anything could be. However, they were never confused as to the fact that Jesus was the Savior who had properly earned their devotion and worship through his teachings, his claims and miracles. But what would life without him look like? And more importantly, how would they advance and sustain the impact and spiritual deposits that Jesus had made throughout the land of Israel and beyond. Also, how would the worship of God proceed after that Jesus had himself returned to his father? In other words, how would their worship of God proceed henceforth? Jesus himself was never silent concerning how God's people should go about the business of worship. Not only did he teach his disciples and many of his hearers some invaluable lessons about worship and how to go about it the proper way, he also lived a life of worship throughout his ministry on earth. Richard C. Leonard made the following observation concerning Jesus and worship,

> "…Jesus was a consistent worshiper, not only through his life of prayer in the presence of the Father, but also through his participation in the formal worship of his Jewish community. He attended festivals in Jerusalem (John 5:1; 7:37) and took his place regularly in the Sabbath assembly of the synagogue (Luke 4:16). Public as well as private worship was important to Jesus, and he had some pointed and specific things to say to his followers about it. And when, after his resurrection, the young church began to assemble regularly, his teaching and example gave shape to the worship of the new community."[12]

Indeed, some of the teachings and acts of Jesus significantly bring out the huge importance that he

---

[12] R.C. Leonard, "A sensible approach to Christian truth"

attached not only to the act and method of worship, but also to the value placed on the place of worship. For example, as earlier mentioned when Jesus acted to chase away the traders that had turned the temple into a market place, he sought to create awareness of the fact that the place of worship required as much attention as the worshipers and as such must not be treated with disrespect and disdain. (Matthew 21) He knew his Scriptures well and that the temple was indeed a sacred space where God's presence truly dwelt and as such must be treated with a high degree of reverence. Few other references in the Scriptures demonstrate Jesus' concern for everything pertaining to the worship of his father as the incident cited above. Again concerning this point Leonard observes that "The purity of the earthly place of worship was important to him, or he would not have taken the drastic action of cleansing the temple".[13] The author further points out that "Jesus stood in the biblical tradition which recognizes that certain geographic spots have a sacred quality, as places where God has made himself known in a special way."[14]

One more example where Jesus showed great concern towards attitude and character in worship was in his encounter with the Samaritan Woman at the Well. In a conversation with that unusual and ordinary woman Jesus debunked generationally held misconceptions about worship, thereby drawing attention to the type

---

[13] R.C. Leonard
[14] Ibid

Worshiping Disorders

of worship acceptable to God. It would help to quote extensively the content of this important exchange.

> [20] Our fathers worshiped on this mountain, but you say that in Jerusalem is the place where people ought to worship."[21] Jesus said to her, "Woman, believe me, the hour is coming when neither on this mountain nor in Jerusalem will you worship the Father.[22] You worship what you do not know; we worship what we know, for salvation is from the Jews.[23] But the hour is coming, and is now here, when the true worshipers will worship the Father in spirit and truth, for the Father is seeking such people to worship him.[24] God is spirit, and those who worship him must worship in spirit and truth." (John 4:20-24).

This encounter was a type of reset, a tutoring for a people stuck in their past and ignorant of the new things that God was doing in the world to bring his people closer to himself. Through it, Jesus laid the foundation for the type of worship that must replace the old thinking, the worship that God requires, thereby setting a standard for not only the early church but also for all generations of Christians to come. This extensive encounter with the Samaritan woman has always stood as a test of true and sincere

Worshiping Disorders

worship for all Christians of all time. Jesus continued with this type of reset in all his encounters with the Pharisees and the Teachers of the Law who constantly sought to advance their old patterns of thinking and challenging Jesus' teaching and acts of kindness in the lives of those he encountered.

The period following Jesus' ascension to heaven left the disciple as well as the emerging church with the task of figuring out just how to be followers and worshipers of God under the new dispensation. As the new faith grew, especially as more of the gentile world embraced it, the problems became more complex. However, one thing remained certain, and that was that the passion among the new community of believers to worship their God was never diminished. They huddled together in house fellowships where they broke Bread and exhorted one another in "Psalms and hymns and spiritual songs", singing and making melody in their hearts to the Lord (Ephesians 5:19). We also learned from the Scriptures that there was a strong spirit of unity and mutual distribution of resources among the believers. (Acts 4:32-35). In other words, as a worshiping community, everybody cared for everybody thereby completely eliminating the spirit of selfishness and greed.

Worship was an accommodating experience which recognized the needs of the very least of the members of the community. For example, on one occasion when the minority Hellenist women were being neglected in the daily distribution of food, the twelve disciples quickly stepped up to their leadership role by immediately appointing seven wise men to oversee that aspect of the church's life to free them up to administer prayer and the Word (Acts 4:1-7). By doing so, order and decency were immediately restored to the church and service and worship to God progressed without hitches. In fact, worship was the glue that held the vulnerable early church together.

The early church wholeheartedly embraced the sacraments which were either commanded by Jesus or introduced by the apostles or their immediate successors. This followed after the practices in the Jewish synagogues that helped to give shape and inspiration to the worship life of the early believers. These believers both Jews and the new gentile entrants into the new faith believed that Jesus was the Savior, the Messiah sent to redeem the world. They regarded him as God-come-down, and made no secret of their veneration of him. They gathered around the Table to celebrate the Lord's Supper in obedience to his "remember me" injunction at the Upper room. In addition, they believed strongly in the authority of his name and consequently prayed therewith as he earlier declared concerning his name, (John 14:14).

The worship of the early church was totally 'Christocentric', that is Christ-centered. It provides several antecedents to the worship of the church as it is practiced today both in form and character. The demand to both worship God and to do so in spirit and truth still stands for every believer. Also, the demand to bring the highest level and quality of worship still goes out to the church today as it did both to our Jewish predecessors and to the early church of Jesus Christ. After all, the Apostle Paul enjoined the church in Corinth that …all things be done decently and in order." (1Corinthians 14:40). Thus, when in our day the church is characterized by all manner of disorderly conducts during worship services, we are in clear departure from the reverential worship practices of past worshipers of the same God we claim to worship today.

PERSPECTIVES AND POSTURES IN WORSHIP

*Come, let us bow down in worship,
let us kneel before the L<small>ORD</small> our Maker;
(Psalm 95:6)*

Historically, Christians have heeded the call by the Psalmist to both kneel and bow before the Lord in worship with absolute obedience and great enthusiasm. These as well as several other physical gestures as raising and clapping of hands, prostrating and on occasion falling flat on the ground as practiced in many worship cultures had been deployed as ways of honoring and worshiping the Christian God. However, the use of much of these gestures appears to have significantly dwindled in much of contemporary Christian worship. This could be attributed mainly to the ferocious attack of post-modern influences, as already discussed in the introduction. The situation is so critical that in some churches, oddity seems to have taken the place of normalcy. In some cases it seems inappropriate and unfashionable to raise one's hands; to kneel or to prostrate during worship and prayer in congregations where these gestures are generally not viewed as normal practice. But the call to deploy such gestures in worship is a scriptural one which ought to be seen as inclusive and not culturally or denominational discriminatory among believers.

Worshiping Disorders

One may therefore begin to question the rationale behind the toning down or in many cases, the complete disappearance of such motions. Has the biblical mandate been seemingly altered or perhaps out rightly withdrawn? Or better put, might it be that God no longer cares about such courtesies from his children? Put in another way, are Christians losing some sense of the majesty of the one whom they once revered and adored? Any suggestion that in our time God no longer cares about such gestures as called out in Scriptures will be grossly misleading and far from the truth. Where such gestures have been abandoned, it is either that worshipers have become insanely too aware of themselves thereby considering bowing or prostrating too dishonorable or insulting to their person, or have simply become unwittingly austere towards God with their heads, limbs and voices.

Christians of old had knees that were bendable; they had heads that were 'bowable' and they had hands that were 'raiseable'. Today Christians have knees that are either too stiff or too precious to hit the floor in adoration and honor of their Lord. Their necks have become too stiff and their hands hang down as though disabled by medical incapacity. But these very same people are often prepared to break those same rules when they encounter certain people of high social standing - people of influence and affluence from whom they expect some earthly benevolences. Such people often referred to as "VIPs" and the "who's whos" in the society; attract the unmitigated services of praise-singers that sometimes include the very same people who would not bow in deference to the creator of all things.

Apart from every human attitude in the 21st century however, the Psalmist's call to bow and kneel before the Lord God our maker remains as urgent and as relevant as ever. Worshiping God with our bodily gestures communicate far more than anyone can ever imagine, hence the call to do so.

Cultural Perspectives

It is important to mention that deploying observable bodily motion and courtesies in worship is not exclusive to Christian worship. In his book titled, *Worship As Body Language* (1997), Elochukwu E. Uzukwu examines the power of bodily courtesies as a way of communicating honor and respect to important personalities in a number of societies in some countries especially in the West African sub-region. His studies among some Nigerian ethnic groups show that a young Yoruba or Nupe would 'sink' to the ground or 'prostrate full-length' before an elder. Similarly, the Urhobos revered the elder by touching the ground with both hands. Also among the Akan of the neighboring Ghana, subjects would pull off their shoes when going into the presence of the 'Asantehene' (king).

This author is privileged to be of Igbo extraction in the South-Eastern part of the West African nation of Nigeria. There is a popular expression from that region namely, "Igbo enwe eze" meaning, "Igbo's have no kings." However, in spite of that generally-held belief, respect for the elderly and for the ancestors remains very deep-rooted. The elders and men and women of title have continued to enjoy their pride of place in the Igbo society to this day. As a matter of fact, in most strongly traditional locales of Igboland, the words of the 'Igwe's (the Chiefs) or 'Ndichie's or the 'Ikengas', (the Chief's counselors) remain final. It is generally believed that these traditional leaders provide living connections to the departed ancestors. Concerning the Igbos, Omenka Egwuatu Nwa-Ikenga (2011), observed, "The Igbo people have understood the importance of honoring the *Ndichie* (Venerated ancestors) in order for the civilization to survive and progress from times immemorial. One of the reasons Igbos and Africans in general are in a state of damnation is because we have forgotten how to honor our ancestors."[15]

Using the term "damnation" to describe the consequence of not respecting the Igbo ancestors is a very strong word indeed. However, it is a word that seems to capture the seriousness of the situation within the Igbo traditional worship systems. From the foregoing, we can understand that honoring the ancestors is so fundamental in the Igbo cultural consciousness that failure to do so it is believed, evokes supernatural repercussions. In the not so distant past, idol worshipers in my native town of

---

[15] Omenka Egwuatu Nwa-Ikenga, "Honoring The Ancestors"

Ngwo demonstrated high levels of reverence, servitude and fear for the 'ezemmuo' (the high priest) of their shrines and were extremely careful about the way they behaved before him lest calamity came calling.

A look at some other religions also reveals some significant things within those religions. For example, the Islamic religion's deployment of body gestures and rituals often convey a high degree of reverence to the deity that they venerate. During worship they, as a matter of compulsory ritual, pull off their shoes and perform some observable body movements including washing of some body parts before entering the mosque to pray. Moreover, the choreographed movement of their liturgical prayer portrays such an artistic beauty that it arguably, attracts the attention of a large segment of curious admirers. On occasion, some of these admirers especially from the very curious Western world even go a step further to embrace the Islamic religion, attracted by the dramatic liturgical movements.

Body movements and sacred rituals belong generally together, irrespective of whatever circumstances they meet. Consequently, one can safely conclude that worship rituals in addition to creating an atmosphere of sacredness, which elevates the god-image in the worshiper, is also capable of ultimately bringing an aesthetic value to the worship event itself. In other words, sacred movements have a way of bringing beauty and unity to a worship event. Elochukwu further notes that, "because worship is concerned with body motions or gestures, African Christians see worship as a channel to display their deep experience of the mystery revealed in the Christian story."[16] But this is not all. He sees a possible direct link between bodily gestures in worship and ethical behaviors afterwards. Studies in ritual action, he suggests, has revealed that religious practice has ethical implications.

But how would ethics and morality come into a conversation about physical gestures in worship? If we agree with Elochukwu's argument that religious practice or ritual does indeed play out in the ways and manners in which people conduct their lives, then it would be easy to see just why Christians have generally lost it in their worship behaviors, with sometimes unintended consequences on their willingness to continue to subscribe to biblical demands for a holy living before a holy God. In other words, it appears that whenever these open gestures and acts that have the capacity to at least commandeer immediate and observable allegiance to God are denied, a significant aspect of who we are as a worshiping community may be largely compromised.

Oftentimes too, reluctance on the outward can point to the coldness in the inward. When a worshiper releases all to the Holy Spirit, not one single part of the individual is spared from the influence of the

---

[16] Elochukwu E. Uzoukwu, "Worship As Body Language", p.15, 19.

spirit. On the contrary, when worship is in the flesh, a person soon suddenly realizes like Adam and Eve that he or she is naked. When once worship lacks the full control of the spirit therefore, all that is left is a whitewash; a gathering akin to just about a gathering in a movie theater or a town hall meeting. It is not difficult to see the effects of the increasing disappearance of etiquette and decorum among Christian worshipers with Christians appearing to feel near to nothing of the mystery and awe which the sanctuary of worship once inspired among believers.

J.G. Davies (1973) takes this very subject to yet another level when he observes that worship rituals symbolize values and lead to commitment. He writes, "In any act of worship, there is not just an amalgam of separation, transition and incorporation…there is also an accompanying moral commitment to the values declared."[17] Understood within the context of our discussion therefore, appropriate movements and rituals would help instill a sense of sacredness on all present, thereby triggering a readiness to assume responsibility to worship God in the proper way and with the proper character. This point probably calls attention to Jesus' words, "The hour is coming and has now come when the true worshipers will worship the Father in the Spirit and in truth" (John 4: 23). When we bring all of what we are, into our worship, spirit, soul, and body, the possibility of being conscious of our moral character while standing

---

[17] J. G. "Davies, "Every Day God", p. 268.

before the holy God is more likely to significantly increase.

Worship calls for all of who we are. The human body is created to be an instrument of worship. Our hands, feet, mouths, heads and indeed every part of our being are all designed to perform what Dawn (1995) refers to as 'movements of adoration' or 'gestures of sacredness' and postures of virtue.'[18] Failure to deploy any of those parts in the worship and pleasuring of God (Revelation 4:11) negates the purpose for which they were created. This negligence amounts to a serious disorder, if disorder is defined in terms of something that loses its capacity to play the role for which it was fashioned in an adequate manner. What can be more out of order than when Christians forcefully keep what belongs to God from serving the purposes for which they are created? In the view of Robert, Webber (1985), bodily gestures "are not mere external trappings, but are ways of bringing external actions in line with internal feelings."[19] Therefore, when we keep our hands from rising towards the heavens; when we keep our feet from dancing; when we keep our mouths from singing and shouting the 'halleluiahs' and 'amens', we may have been inflicted with a terrible disease whose name is called ingratitude.

---

[18] Dawn, p.267.
[19] Webber, p.107.

Theological Perspectives

("To the unknown god" (Acts 17:23)

In Acts of the Apostles chapter 17, the Athenians were doing their very best in the worship of a god that was unknown to them. Because they did not know that god, they offered him a highly fractured worship. The apostle Paul sought to bring them to the awareness that they had been engaging in a meaningless exercise. They had a wrong understanding of who the real God was and so were worshiping him as though he dwelt in "temples made with hands" (vs.24), or as the text put it, worshiped "with men's hands as though he needed anything". Could the Christians of today be worshiping an Unknown God? Current developments in Christian worship services demand that we examine some basic biblical perspectives on the subject. That worship has increasingly become a victim of an 'anything goes' society is a fact so well known. God's people have become increasingly careless in approaching his presence, a fact which makes it pertinent to examine the things that may have been compromised. I strongly believe that our understanding of God may have suffered a huge setback. Studies in contemporary Christian worship indicate that many Christians appear to be fast losing the picture of the majesty of God especially in the face of a highly secularized world.

Worshiping Disorders

In his book titled *Don't Waste your Time in Worship* (1978), James L. Christensen attributes the laissez-faire attitude or what he refers to as 'take-it-or-leave-it indifference' towards worship today as being rooted in secularization of life. He points out that, "If one has no adequate image with which to perceive God and no valid experience of God in his life, it is doubtful that worship will ever be a demanding exercise and, even less, a meaningful experience."[20] Two things stand out here. The first is a person's God-image while the other is the person's personal experience of God. A person who has experienced the hand of God will hold God with the highest reverence while a purposeless worshiper will approach God with utmost disregard.

Dawn (1995) also points out that the fearfulness of God must be held in dialectal tension with his mercy and love in order for us to truly experience the genuine "fear and love" of God which she adjudges to be more than awe and reverence. Only when this balance is established can we "bow before the mystery and never treat our relationship to God with flippancy."[21] There is no doubt that when Christians behave in odd ways at worship, it is a sign that "Not only the church but God himself is 'dumbed down', made too small, trivialized."[22] A person whose understanding of God is shallow can only be said to be worshiping an unknown god even if the person

---

[20] Christensen, p. 19.
[21] Dawn, p.97.
[22] Ibid.

Worshiping Disorders

thinks it is Yahweh that is being worshiped.

Understanding is very fundamental in getting it right in worship. Worship that recognizes the majesty and awesomeness of the presence of God leaves the worshiper reeling in an unforgettable supernatural experience of the presence of God. No true encounter with God in worship ever leaves both God and the worshipers the same. The worshiper is struck by the overpowering beauty of God's holiness and of his divine majestic presence often manifested by ways of inexplicable joy, peace and reassurances of God's love, while on his own part God enjoys the heartfelt reverence, honor and wholesome adoration of his children on earth. When praises and heartfelt worship go up to heaven, God becomes fearful and begins to do wonders. (Exodus 15:11). In other words, whenever praises go up, salvation, blessings, healings, etc comes down in abundance, for God himself had said that "Whoso offereth praise glorifieth me: and to him that ordereth his conversation aright will I shew the salvation of God, (Psalm 50:23 KJV).

All through the Scriptures, every time people came in contact with God, they were struck by God's awesome presence and the result was always that such persons bowed down, fell on their knees or out rightly fell on the ground and worshiped. When people encounter God, the presence and glory of God would not enable them to act in ways that are familiar or normal. No 'normal' behavior can indeed be expected from anyone who collides with God's manifold presence. God ordered Moses in Exodus. 3:5 to take off his shoes because the place he was standing was holy ground. There was fear; there was awe, but such fear and awe were good and desirable ones. Moses knew he had encountered one far greater than him. Moses encountered sights he had never seen before in his life. For the first time since creation, human eyes saw the wonders of a bush on fire but whose leaves were not being consumed. That's what it feels like sometimes when we encounter God's presence. Awesome and supernatural wonders happen!

At the dedication of Solomon's temple, the officiating ministers (the priests) could not enter the temple they came to dedicate because the glory of God was way too intense for them. The worshipers felt His overwhelming presence saturate the whole temple. The best they could do was to go on their knees on the pavement "with their faces on the ground." (2Chronicles 7:3). There they managed to offer their worship to God. Here we see that God is very tangibly present in his house. His children worshiped him tangibly, with undivided attention, with purpose and reverence and with a high sense of exaltation in their hearts.

In the New Testament the disciples gathered in one accord in Jerusalem in anticipation of the promise of visitation from the Holy Spirit. The spirit of the Lord eventually descended on them like a mighty rushing wind, bringing with him a holy confusion such that the world had never known before. Tongues of fire rested on each head while each spoke in languages not previously learned. When this holy 'drama' ended, we have what we know today as the day of Pentecost, the day when a single encounter with God produced for God's people all over the world a Comforter, Helper, Teacher and Encourager. There is indeed no telling the degree of benevolence that descends on people who bring down God's glory in worship. On the contrary, emptiness fills the atmosphere where people turn God's house into a playroom where God is dishonored and disrespected.

King David said to God in Psalm 63:2; "I have seen you in the sanctuary and beheld your power and your glory." If God's glory and power are in the sanctuary of worship, why should a worshiper or a group of the same hold worship with such contempt and disdain? God's people noticeably do in the sanctuary of worship things they would not dare to do in regulated public spaces. When people display certain inappropriate behaviors at such places sanctions often follow. For example, people who misbehave in judicial law courts face prosecution for 'contempt of court' with appropriate punishments meted out to them. When people flout restriction orders on the use of certain prohibited items such as mobile phones and other communication gadgets in airplanes, military installations or hospitals, they suffer appropriate severe sanctions. This makes one to wonder whether Christians who display disorderly and uncivil acts in God's house ever realize that they can be liable to contempt or sanction? Or does it not amount to contempt of worship to trample on the majesty of the Almighty God? Can anything indeed be more contemptible than to disturb proceedings during the acts of worship of God's people? Or perhaps one may question what right anyone possibly has to engage in acts that desecrate a piece of property which Jesus himself has claimed as his father's house? As such, very many Christian worshipers are unwittingly, repeat offenders because of the unruly behavior they display at worship gatherings or even during their personal worship practices.

Quite often, we bask under the knowledge that God lays no immediate charges on anyone, but rather lovingly invites all violators to repentance. So God's people sometimes press God's grace so hard. King Solomon's charge to Israel is noteworthy, "Guard your steps [Stand in awe of God] when you go to the house of God. Go near to listen rather than to offer the sacrifice of fools, who do not know what they do wrong." [Ecclesiastes. 5:1]. Doesn't Solomon's injunction imply that some people are oblivious of the fact that they behave irreverently in God's sanctuary? God rebuked Israel through the Prophet Jeremiah for improper acts of worship despite which they still "come and stand before me in this house which bears my name and say, "We are safe"-safe to do all these detestable things?" [Jeremiah 7:10]. In addition, David enjoins Israel to "Give unto the Lord the glory due His name; Worship the Lord in the beauty of his holiness" [Psalm 29:2]. The call for the worshipers of God to behave appropriately before him is very prominent throughout the Scriptures and that call is no less resounding in our day.

One thing is very clear from all that have been discussed in this chapter; God is, as he has always been, interested in what goes on in his house. No one must continue to feel 'safe' to do detestable things in the house of worship. Christian worshipers must begin to recognize the majestic presence of God in his house. They must begin to understand what God meant when he told Moses out of the burning yet unconsumed bush that the place he was standing was 'holy ground'. Christian worshipers must differentiate between the church and the movie theatre. Christians must learn or relearn reverence to the majestic God of creation. That is the way all true children of God have always done business with God. That is what Jesus himself announced when he encountered the woman at the well. On that occasion, he announced the arrival of a time when all worship that is unspiritual and untruthful will be decisively rejected by his father who seeks only worship that is both spiritual and true. [John 4:23]. That time is now!

Concluding Remarks

I have in all the preceding chapters discussed worship as a sacred duty handed down to Christians of the 21st century by the men and women who God called out to do so. I also pointed out that reverence; decorum and civility seem to be missing in present day Christian worship practices and these diminish

Worshiping Disorders

commitment to wholly fulfill the call to worship. Of great concern is exposing the hindrances that challenge the ability of Christians to fulfill this call What are the pitfalls, the enemies that we are up and against in our efforts to be true and effective worshipers?

In the chapters that follow, I will attempt to identify and discuss in detail some of these hindrances and pitfalls. I will be looking at such disruptive misconducts as lateness, phone interferences during worship, loitering and restless behaviors, sleeping during services, casual posturing and over relaxation during services, eating during services, dressing for church, quitting service prematurely etc. It is the manifestations of attitudes such as these and several other such behaviors that I have chosen to refer to as "Worshiping Disorders". I consider these as disorders because they are importations, satanic institutions of some sort; and they are the consequences of post-modern lackadaisical mindsets and attitudes that deny respect both for God and people. These behaviors are, to say the least, the spoilers of Christian worship in our generation. That is not to say that our generation is exclusive in experiencing acts such as these. But, few past generations of Christian worshipers have ever experienced worship misbehaviors to the levels that we see today with the uncontrollable proliferation of churches around the world. It is some of these misbehaviors that we now turn our attention to.

Worshiping Disorders

THE PROBLEM OF LATENESS

Many readers of this book might remember the days when people took matters of punctuality to church services and Christian events very seriously. I remember when my late mother, along with very many others would wake up when the first early morning warning church bells would announce to the entire village that they had barely thirty minutes to hurry to the village church for morning meditation to start the day. When once that happened, all church goers ensured that they made their ways to the church early enough to beat the final round of the bell which announced that service had begun. During those days, it was quite unusual to treat time for worship as though it mattered nothing, and people who lived at the time would shudder at ways those living today have generally chosen to treat time.

The decision therefore, to put the issue of lateness, also referred to as 'tardiness', first on the list of disorders in Christian worship to be discussed in this book is not a random one. Rather, it is a deliberate decision made for a number of reasons. First, it has become an increasingly noticeable, recurring and endemic attitude in many circles especially in worship activities thereby constituting a great embarrassment both to the culprits and to God. Second, it is a habit that very often, if left unchecked is capable of

Worshiping Disorders

seriously hurting other people who are also involved in the drama of everyday life. For persons who have suffered from the often avoidable consequences of lateness, it is one habit to be dealt with at all costs. Sadly, it is easier said than done. Lateness is an issue of somewhat crisis proportions in the community to which I belong namely, the African community. To say the least, it is both shameful and disorienting and thus will not be treated with kid's gloves in this chapter. Hopefully, this book will help to make all persons who are caught up in this bad behavior to have a rethink and urgently turn around and away from it. I will begin with a definition.

What is Lateness?

According to the Cambridge Dictionary of English, lateness is defined as "Doing something" or something "taking place after the expected, proper or usual time". In other words, when a person or event falls behind the scheduled time slot of its start, it is said to start late. In addition, when a person or event doesn't end when it was scheduled to end, it is said to end late. Thus, a person is considered guilty of lateness when they fail to show a lack of promptness to an event. The Latin origins of the word, 'tardy' which is 'tardus' meaning, "slow, sluggish, dull, or stupid" says volumes about the root causes of this very habit. The opposite of lateness is 'punctual' which is defined as "Happening or doing something at the agreed or proper time."

A vast number of people often demonstrate serious problems when it comes to being punctual to events. The problem appears only to be getting increasingly worse by the day as many more involvements place their demands on people's scarce time. Despite this challenge, being punctual or late to a scheduled event lies squarely on the shoulders of each and every individual. Notable writers have written many books and articles on the issue of habitual lateness and time management. Some of these writers even used their personal struggles with lateness to illustrate how damaging this habit could be. They also discussed how they overcame the habit all in a bid to help those still within its grip. However, it does appear that many people still manufacture more excuses to remain trapped in the habit. But it is one issue to which this book seeks to make a significant contribution because it is a problem that has made a strong inroad into the church with sometimes grave consequences. This is one problem concerning which very few people can claim righteousness. As you read this book, all those who struggle with this problem must humbly and prayerfully look to God for help. In other words, there should be no finger-pointing towards another person without self-examination in this matter.

It is a Matter of Choice

Being late or not to an event is a choice. However, it is expected that when someone willfully assent or commits to an invitation, it is incumbent on the person to honor the time scheduled for that event. Therefore by choosing to commit to an event and then showing up at one's convenience instead of the scheduled time, one treats the organizers of the event very unfairly and with disrespect. Such attitude smacks of selfishness and wanton disregard for civility and decorum. Unfortunately, this attitude - an attitude that generally reflects the spirit of the present age - persists in some Christian circles especially among some African churches in the Diaspora. It is a habit quite often repudiated by all people of integrity and quality. This leaves one to wonder how any Christian could justify the habit of lateness to the house of worship. Is it a matter of formed habits, or simply a matter of values? Or is it perhaps a result of something else beyond human control?

This brings us to the second point which is that one's attitude to punctuality really depends on one's understanding of, and the value placed on the activity. Put another way, for worshipers, it depends on a person's motivation for going to church. For some people, going to church might simply be regarded as an extension of their day's social engagements where they catch up with friends following a long week of busyness. For others, it provides a sort of break to the loneliness of their day especially in more modern and cosmopolitan societies where life has become egalitarian. There are many who see church events as obligations bequeathed on them through parental heritage albeit against their will. Yet many others view it as a privileged invitation to have fellowship with their creator and with their spiritual siblings, an invitation to which they respond appropriately with thankfulness and a sense of elation. Such people often belong in the minority. However, they often come to the Sanctuary with a strong sense of, anticipation and responsibility. People in this category can barely wait for the next worship opportunity to arrive. Like King David, they are always glad to go to the house of the Lord and to go there as and when due. (Psalm 122:1.)

"Better Late than Never": One easily recognizable expression to most people who will read this book is the phrase "Better late than never"! This phrase stands conspicuously on billboards around the world. It is printed on car stickers and printed on pamphlets and photo frames hanging in people's living rooms. People grow up to either embrace or reject its appeal and philosophy. Its appeal sounds all so true, but behind the idea hides a subtle encouragement to make lateness a lifestyle. In a sense, this jargon has become every habitual late comer's catch phrase of self-delusion and appeasement. It justifies tardiness and encourages lousiness. It is one philosophy that is quite often exploited especially when a person has no personal stakes in an event. On the contrary, when people have appointments and dates that are of particular personal interest they more often than not never show up late. Most people who travel either by air, sea, rail or road would not be late to the departure terminals. In fact, air travel often requires presence at the ports of departure at least two to three hours to departure time depending on one destination and check-in requirements. Failing to show up and complete the process causes one to suffer some inconvenience and financial loss.

Ironically, on some occasions lateness is not viewed with such degree of seriousness especially if the latecomer fails to see the seriousness attached to the appointment as the person on the other side, or if they risk no personal loss. Such people often have an "it-doesn't-really-matter" attitude. In their mind, the event can always go on with or without their presence. Quite unfortunately, such also becomes the case with church services and events. To them, the service will most certainly proceed as planned irrespective of who is present and who is not. God would accuse no one of lateness since he is physically invisible. The leadership of the church may accept the excuses provided or not even bother to discipline depending on the environment.

Some worshipers even think it is no one's business what time they come to church. Such individualistic thinking appears therefore to strengthen the propensity of many to go even deeper in matters of tardiness. In Africa and as in much of emerging civilizations, church authorities still enjoy the audacity to exercise some form of disciplinary measures over erring members. However, in the Diaspora, many immigrant worshipers who attend church services often choose to exercise their freedom to come late to church events without any remorse or apologies to anyone including the same God they claim to

Worshiping Disorders

worship! People like those often feel no sense of accountability or responsibility towards anyone. The following anonymous online quote voices the frustration of one commentator on this serious question of lateness in the church:

> "Know this today, anytime you go to Church one minute late, you have NOT attended Church at all. There is a register of God, where angels record the name of those who come on time, and you'll be surprised that in Heaven they will tell you, you never attended Church. If Christ is saying 'where two or three are gathered, I'm in their midst', you think He comes late?"[23]

Clearly, this claim can be viewed as a rather extreme and radical one on the subject; yet it appears to capture a widely but scripturally unsubstantiated view held by many. However, few readers can argue against the fact that God is always present in the gathering of his people with the highest degree of seriousness which in turn demands our response likewise term, and he never shows up late because with God there is no such concept as lateness! It makes sense then to almost subscribe to the idea that those who come after the appointed time most

---

[23] Naijasky, "The Danger of Lateness to Church"

certainly disadvantage themselves in unquantifiable ways.

The Fallacy of "African Time":

The issue of lateness is so prevalent and deeply ingrained within entire communities that it has come to be a defining identity for many. For example, a vast majority of Africans appear to have overwhelmingly subscribed to the doctrine of "African time". Yes, "African time!" We are talking here about a fallacy, a very dirty garment that an entire community chose to put on themselves and publicly brag about. The concept of 'African time' is an evil and destructive doctrine that is so clearly evident in every facet of activity among the majority of Africans that people have become very unapologetic about it. It is one big lie that appears to have come to colonize the mentality of a whole generation of Africans. It is an aberration, an outright misnomer that has come to be nearly totally embraced and celebrated. At home as in the Diaspora, this doctrine runs so deep. It traverses private as well as public lifestyles. Its manifestation cuts across every type of human activity so that no event is ever expected to begin on the scheduled time. Event organizers plan in upwards of two to three hours, sometimes four of lateness to every event as a standard, knowing that invitees are fully aware of the prevalent and unwritten time code within the community.

For example, if something as serious as a wedding

Worshiping Disorders

service is to begin at 12.00, the time on the invitation card will read 9.00 or 10.00. This provision for lateness is known as "African time", to which both the organizers and the invitees instinctively accommodate. Anyone who came at the time written on the invitation is considered pedantic and foolish. This evil philosophy is so ingrained that it colonizes and assaults the intelligence of the high and the lowly, punishing the subscriber and the non-subscriber alike. The manner of this punishment is based on the fact that invitees to a function who value and keep to time are usually subjected to excruciating ordeals of having to wait for hours before the events actually commence. In most cases, many of the invitees arrive at the venue with the host/hostess nowhere to be found. In very extreme cases, some guests take their leave out of frustration after long and hopeless waits thereby missing out on the event altogether. This shameless flaunting of lateness often creates a nightmare particularly for guests who had planned other activities on the same day. They are torn between remaining a part of the late event and cancelling other events, or leave all other things they had planned to do altogether. This, quite unfortunately, is a lifestyle that very many people have to adjust to.

It is the height of incivility to take other people for granted; It is the height of incivility to waste other people's time and to disregard their right to attend other activities they had planned to do because you arrive or start late to a scheduled event. In some cases, the functionaries come late to events and people have to wait for them. By all possible imaginations, this evil philosophy of 'African time' has all the trappings of a collective stigma from which all well-meaning people must now seek to extricate themselves, albeit forcefully and very determinedly.

Perhaps, the greatest worry is the extent to which lateness has found its way into the church. This is because if it is a big problem with regard to social events, it is by far a much greater problem for the church. If it does no significant damage to ordinary routines of the daily life of people, it surely has very disruptive effect on the church's life in general with great implications for the worship gathering itself. Whereas a social gathering is purely a 'humans' activity, Christian worship is at all times and places, a solemn appointment with a God who desires that everything be done orderly and decently. Christian worship is a covenant of time of some sort, a deal struck between the worshiped and the worshiper. Consequently, lateness is a behavioral disorder that is motivated by a clear lack of respect by the latter for the former, and as such a flagrant violation of that covenant relationship. This is something that must no longer be given a place at all in all the business of God's people and that due to a number of reasons.

It is even more shocking that when people are late to a worship event, they display no sense of urgency or embarrassment, yet such people would do no such thing in activities they had purchased a ticket to

Worshiping Disorders

attend. For example, when I am late to a movie that is already in progress, I usually rush with every sense of urgency, mindful that I may be missing not only interesting movie trailers, but also very essential opening segments of the movie that I have committed my hard-earned resources to watch. Sometimes that sense of urgency may even suggest the thought of saving up on time by giving up the purchase of snacks and drinks. Sometimes too a person can decide to invest scarce resources in taxi ride than taking the slow-moving public bus in order to catch up with an important appointment. Furthermore, most workers in the public and private sector fully understand what can happen when they report late to work, especially when it becomes habitual. That most employers have zero tolerance for late coming is a fact well known by most employees. In all of the above scenarios, people are willing to take extreme measures to avoid consequential lateness.

However, scarcely would most worshipers take any steps or make the least sacrifices in order to avoid arriving late to a church activity. What often happens instead is the direct opposite. People walk into the sanctuary as though they are on an evening stroll. There is no sense at all that they are indeed violating the communal agreement of a holy community whose time of gathering is well known to all. The decision to worship at a particular time and place is a communal one in which God himself is involved. Therefore, God never gets honored, neither do the rest of the members of that community get encouraged each time violations happen, especially with no demonstrable show of remorse. Rather than being remorseful, quite often, some daring latecomers are audacious enough to stop to exchange pleasantries with their fellow culprits and sometimes with those already well-seated before finally breaking in through the pews, thereby distracting everyone along their path. The fact that worship is already in progress may have no restraining effect on their attitude. It is as if they take great pride in showing up late. Some people have actually suggested that some folks come late with the intent to make a noticeable entrance into the church for the purpose of showing off their beautiful clothing to the admiration of those already seated. Whether this is simply a myth or a reality will be left to each reader's judgment.

The church has struggled with this problem for far too long. I remember a number of other myths similar to the one I quoted earlier that were peddled around during my early years as a Christian, all aimed at instilling fear for lateness in people with a view to curbing the habitual practice of lateness to church events. This particular myth had it that the angels of God often stood as sentries by the entrances to the sanctuary, waiting with packages of blessings for people who are punctual to church worship services. Once the angels were done distributing the blessings to all who have merited it as reward for their punctuality they vanished with the undelivered packages. This is yet one more claim that cannot be authenticated by Scripture. Consequently, we must view it as yet one more of those motivational efforts aimed at combating the scourge of lateness in the church.

Two things are very obvious here though. First, God does indeed honor those that honor him. As pointed out earlier, fellowship times are sacred appointments. There is no doubt that rewards await those who respect the timings of those appointments. But on the other hand, there must also be a cost for those who are in habitual violation of the rules of engagement and who display a nonchalant attitude towards such timings as collectively agreed to. The truth is that like most acts of indiscipline, lateness also attracts some very sad consequences. God comes to us at times and circumstances of his own choosing. During times of divine visitation, heaven waits for no one regardless of the reason for late arrivals. When God comes around, he benefits those on their duty posts in powerful and verifiable ways. A few examples will be necessary to illustrate this point. In chapter one of the gospel of Luke, Zacharias received an angelic visitation that ended the childless condition between him and Elizabeth his wife. The good news came to him, "While he was performing his priestly service before God in the *appointed* order of his division…according to the custom of the priestly office…." (Luke 1:8a-9a). We can deduce from this text that this epiphany took place without prior notification. Zacharias was at the right place at the right time. God's appointed time has no accommodation for a person's 'disappointed time', if

Worshiping Disorders

I may put it that way. Consequently, Zacharias may have missed this blessing and Bible history may not have been just the same had he displayed the attitude that many display today.

Another example worthy of mention is the event on the day of Pentecost (Acts 2). The disciples understood that there was a promised Holy Spirit. They kept the injunction to wait in Jerusalem until the day of fulfillment of that promise. But what they were not told was the day and time of the manifestation of the promise. If it were today, several of the disciples may have missed out on the fulfillment of that promise on account of late arrival to the venue. We can remain as positive as possible that no serious disciple of Christ missed out on that great event due to late arrival since the Bible did not say otherwise. Pentecost remains a continuing experience of God's people however, and it is very sad to know that lack of punctuality continues to deny many Christians of their divine blessings. There is clearly no such thing as reserved portions for late comers once the Holy Spirit begins his work in the corporate gathering of God's people. Blessings are poured out on all who are present.

Lateness is a gross act of indiscipline, a behavior which is very strange in heaven. That behavior never gets rewarded under any circumstance because God always frowns at any habitual acts of sinfulness and degradation of the human character. A God who is historically known for his prompt interventions in people's lives and situations desires that his children who are made after his image display a similar character of promptness and integrity. Consequently, no provisions are made for offenders in matters of tardiness in any environment where God's presence dwells. The soul therefore, that requires the touch of heaven has the sole responsibility to be well-positioned and to be in good time at the agreed times of the gathering of God's family.

The final example I will mention is the regrettable but illustrated case of the five foolish virgins in Jesus' parable of the Ten Virgins (Matthew 25). In this parable, a clear distinction is made between foolishness and wisdom. The wise exercised the power of discretion while the foolish looked the other way. It is true that the basic lesson Jesus taught in this parable was really not about punctuality or lateness, yet it can be clearly seen that it was a clear lack of discretion or foresight on the part of the foolish five that caused their lateness to the banquet resulting in the door slamming against them. In that sense, a classical lesson on the dangers of lateness also stood out. As one source rightly observed, "Everyone has been late to something at some point, often due to unforeseen or unavoidable circumstances."[24] Unfortunately, the person who usually comes late may pay some form of price or the other, even if there is a justification for the lateness. Perhaps, as you read this, you may remember one or more occasions when you

---

[24] "What does the Bible say about being late or lateness?"

have had to pay a huge and painful price for showing up late for something of immense importance to you. From missing a flight, turning up late for a life-changing job interview, arriving late to an examination or expensive driving test, hospital appointment or perhaps simply watching a bus or train you desperately needed to catch slam its doors against you thereby causing you untold lateness to an important appointment. Whatever, your own experience may have been, many people have felt that pain and disappointment with regrettable consequences.

When we look at all of the above examples, we can almost invariably conclude that receiving the blessings of God has so much to do with timing. As pointed out earlier, God chooses the days and times of his visitation to his people. After all, Ecclesiastes 3:1 says that "To everything there is a season, a time for every purpose under heaven." There is a classical illustration of that in John's Gospel Chapter 5. The incident took place in the city of Jerusalem by the pool of Bethesda. By the five porches of this pool lay several people afflicted with varying types of sicknesses all waiting for the divine moving of the water. An angel of the Lord went down "at a certain time" (vs.4), into the pool and stirred up the water, causing healing on the one who stepped in first. In other words, anyone who missed this time of visitation also missed a chance to be made well. Lateness obviously has untold implications for anyone who has embraced it willfully or otherwise. But it creates great difficulties and inconveniences for other people as well. Someone somewhere usually pays the price for a person's lateness. As the source (Gotquestion.org) referred to above again puts it, "For one thing, continual lateness does not express love for others. Forcing others to wait for us time after time is simply rude."[25] Rudeness is clearly not a desirable Christian character, neither is anything that demonstrates disdain for another. Both must therefore be avoided at all costs.

Some Consequences of Lateness on other Churchgoers

a. A person's lateness can cause another person or persons to become vulnerable to anger and thus to sin. When a person who is punctual is forced to wait interminably for others on a personal appointment or planned group event, such may find themselves grumbling, and in extreme cases of longer waits, cursing, swearing and even making unhealthy remarks about the offender. Putting a person's patience under immense strain and test is the general hallmark of latecomers, especially when the offender fails to communicate the possibility and duration of lateness to the person at the other end. Jesus taught his disciples to pray saying, "And lead us not into temptation…." (Matthew 6:13a). When we keep others waiting always, we certainly set them up for temptation, and when we do that, it is called taking another person for granted, something we do not

---

[25] Gotquestions.org, "What does the Bible say about being late?"

wish that other people do to us.

b. Lateness puts a big question mark on a person's integrity and trustworthiness. It is one of the negative virtues that directly challenge a person's claim to maturity and self-respect. Few people take latecomers very seriously irrespective of their positions in society. The cost of a lack of integrity and reliability are very huge for the church. It is usually very difficult to commit any responsibility to a person who is a habitual latecomer, thereby denying the church of valuable human resources. No church can function effectively if worshipers habitually turn up late to activities. This is something key volunteers at church must constantly keep in mind.

c. Parents who come late to events and church services leave two very negative legacies. First, they cause their children to be late to Sunday school classes and planned youth activities. Consequently, not only do the parents miss out on vital segments of the service, they cause their children to do the same as well. In addition, such behavior does frustrate and confuse those who teach Sunday school and who may have prepared lessons and activities tailored towards an estimated number of children. Secondly, they inadvertently teach their children that it is alright to be late to church and other activities. When such is the case, children continue to advance such mindset since it has been legitimized by their parents. No one else is able to teach them otherwise because parental influence is supreme in the life of every child. With this type of attitude, Christian parents fail to take seriously St. Paul's injunction to Titus namely "And you yourself must be an example to them by doing good works of every kind. Let everything you do reflect the integrity and seriousness of your teaching. (Titus 2:7). When parents fail to live by example, the children are led towards the wrong attitudes and values, something that takes its toll on them much later in life. Cathy S. Truett had this kind of point in mind when she titled her best-seller, *It's Better to Build Boys Than Mend Men*.

d. Finally, nothing can be as discouraging to a worship leader and a pastor as when a service has to begin with nearly empty pews. Not only does the leader feel a sense of frustration, the entire mood of the service gets 'dumbed down'. Also, it gets even worse when certain key participants fail to turn up for preparation and prompt kick off of the service. The music usually becomes the first obvious casualty at such times. It is usually a sorry sight when musicians and singers sneak into their positions while people looked on. Similarly, when an usher comes late, people are left to wonder where to turn and so it is when a prayer leader or a Bible reader fails to turn up in good time. Whenever there appears to be a conspiracy of lateness in a church, the entire service suffers because there would never be an opportunity for a proper preparation neither would there be a time for all the participants to pray together before going to lead others. All who have received the trust of the church leadership to play different roles at a worship service must bear these pitfalls in mind, keeping their sights on the words of 1Corinthians 4:2 which says, "Moreover, it is required of stewards that they be found faithful."

It is highly incomprehensible just how God's people do approach holy things with such degree of levity. It is as though people attempt to hold heaven or an entire community of believers to ransom. To behave in such terms, especially when it becomes habitual is to give one's church community a reputation of lateness that it probably does not deserve because the shame of one church is the shame of all. But also, it amounts to giving both the church and the latecomer an identity that has very damaging potential. A church notoriously associated with late starts is usually held in derision by the outsiders and guests to the church. Visitors get very discouraged and are left with very negative impressions about the church. Such impressions do sometimes last for a long time. Christians and all peoples of integrity must desist from this ungodly behavior, especially with regard to the worship of the Most High God, but also in all other circumstances. Punctuality pays, and it always remains the right attitude to have.

Some Helpful Steps to Avoiding Lateness

Before we leave this topic, I recognize that no true Christian would deliberately indulge in the act of personal embarrassment called lateness, or continue to offend God and tarnish the integrity of the church. In that sense I dare to say to everyone who is weak in this area; there is help. Sometimes, discussing about lateness feels like having a mirror which we all look into from time to time to check our appearances. In this gigantic mirror, the faces of many of us appear so it is not my intention at all to be judgmental and self-righteous. Rather, in this book I offer you a couple of helpful tips on how an urgent and desirable change can be achieved by all of us. In doing that I also fully recognize that tardiness can be a long learned dance step far too difficult to abandon but which we can ask God to help us to unlearn.

a. Find an abiding rhythm or structure for your life or family with regard to church activities is an important key to overcoming habitual lateness. As pointed out by a contributor on this subject, "The structure and order of a Sunday morning routine provides a sense of security and stability that promotes the well-being of individuals and family."[26] "Sunday morning" is a day that is constantly waiting to happen in the life of every believer. Consequently, it must cease to come as a surprise. Individuals and families must strike a structure to ensure that late preparation that gives rise to late attendance is eliminated. This involves prior and definitive decisions on the time to wake up, dress up, eat breakfast, get the kids prepared where applicable etc. Avoiding lateness is about good decision-making. God gets honored and the church is blessed when people do just that. Besides, a strong

---

[26] The Canadian Mar Thoma Church Toronto Sunday School Newsletter "Be on time"

sense of organization and achievement over an important aspect of life grips the family that plans ahead of time.

b. Thinking about unforeseen contingencies is another key. These include; possible flat tires, snow on the windshield during winter or flooding during spring rains, Sunday morning traffic congestion and other unforeseen road situations including road maintenance crews and lane diversions, etc. In addition, think about the parking situation in your church. Sometimes difficulties associated with finding a parking space can be so frustrating it causes some people to either return home or join the service way too late. An old saying has it that "a stitch in time saves nine".

c. Families with babies and toddlers must keep in mind those last-minute smelly surprises that often trigger huge sighs and sometimes baby-spanking temptations. Babies, I suppose, instinctively prefer smelly diapers to be kept at home rather than the house of God. Isn't that being considerate on their part? They probably want to let parents concentrate in church. Great kids aren't they! However, if their 'kindness' is not factored in, one should reckon with delays of sometimes unimaginable proportions.

d. Watch out for Sunday morning distractions. The phone calls can wait until service is over. Friends and family members often have no knowledge of things that are top on your priority. Ask them to call later. .

Worshiping Disorders

Others will not give you your space except you take it by force; neither will there ever be a lack of things to compete for your time on Sundays. Laundries can wait until a more opportune time. Church must not always pay the price for a busy week. The weight and price of a busy week must be put on some other activities Town, community or social club meetings are not sufficient to take up your Sunday worship times. The time for worship must be seen as sacred and sacrosanct. Once you do your ultimate best, you are sure to significantly eliminate factors capable of putting you and your family on the deplorable list of late-comers to Christian fellowships, and you will invariably get your dignity back.

e. Finally, churches must take their own necessary steps to ensure prompt and adequate preparations to eliminate any delays in starting and ending services promptly. Equipment managers are usually, in some cases, contributory to late starts of services. The start of the service is not the time to be testing out the microphones or the time for the choir to rehearse their songs. Pastors should also endeavor to avoid all distracting encumbrances coming from parishioners in order to concentrate on the task of preparing for the worship service. I have been to a number of churches that started in upwards of 15 to 25 minutes behind schedule. I once witnessed a very sad incident at a church in Chicago where I attended a service with my friends. In this particular incident, the sermon was held up midway for upwards of 15 minutes simply because the internet from which the local pastor was to beam segments of his sermon as preached by the General Overseer failed. In the end, the problem persisted despite all the efforts by the technical team and his sermon literarily ended. Of course my friends and I chose to never return to that church. We didn't judge the church, but we simply didn't think we could ever put up with such extreme worshiping disorder again!

Delays, especially unwarranted delays such as mentioned above clearly do not speak well of any church. One of the ugliest results of such tardiness is that parishioners and first timers are kept waiting while technicians fiddled with technology, or while people talked and moved around the sanctuary when service ought to have started. In other words, there is no sufficient reason whatsoever for a church service to begin later than planned or held up midway except for clearly unavoidable circumstances that will be obvious to everyone present.

Lateness is a monster with great power of devastation that can only be defeated through God's help, self-discipline, determination and fervent prayer for those who are weak in this area. It is one of the major changes people have to make as a statement of intention to correct some of the behaviors that are very disrespectful to God and his church. It has hurt the churches very much and still does and will continue to do so until every believer cries out to God in contrition and asks for help and power of victory. Now is the time to finally reject this anomaly and reject it overwhelmingly. This rejection is one which must happen both on an individual and corporate scale, for when we are liberated from its clutches on individual levels then the church as a community gets healed.

Worshiping Disorders

THE ABUSE OF MOBILE GADGETS/DEVICES

It was one of the most solemn moments of the worship service that morning. As people were worshiping and were being healed and blessed by the overwhelming and palpable presence of God with many sobbing in deep contrition and spiritual visitation from their Maker, suddenly, one of those untamed mini gadgets from someone's bag or pocket goes off defiantly, and unapologetically. I honestly cannot quite recall the exact ringtone that bellowed out of that device, but the toxicity and repulsiveness of it was surely enough to immediately pollute the spiritual atmosphere of the moment, causing such a negative dissonance for many who were in the meeting. Some worshipers' spiritual ascendancy was immediately interrupted. It was a very monstrous moment, but it was not an isolated incident by any means. It was simply that this time, it appeared particularly audacious, rude and nonsensical while being destabilizing to say the least. Yes, there are limitless words to describe that bizarre moment.

I also clearly recall another worship gathering where one of those tiny gadgets played a real bad game. As the organist was skillfully playing and people were beginning to sink into the rich and solemn lyrics of the great hymn "Amazing grace", a telephone suddenly rings out. It could have been a bit pardonable had the ringtone synced with the chords that were being played. But unfortunately, the music that came was in such disagreement with the chord of the organ that there followed an immediate catharsis, a sort of very painfully negative emotional resolution that left many wondering the need for such electronic intrusions in spiritual affairs. Again, because worshipers are not supposed to be vindictive, no one dared make a racket so the awkward moment passed without any noticeable reaction from anyone. God's people have been successfully assaulted one more time. Such examples are countless. It happens in nearly every church and many other worship gatherings.

Mobile devices have become such a huge problem in the church to almost idolatrous proportions. Unfortunately, it is one problem to which nearly every worship participant shows a lot of unspoken intolerance and disdain. Ironically many of those who show signs of intolerance to this disturbing problem also become culprits themselves on occasion. Such is the power to which these devices hold so many users. It is a practical necessity that holds nearly every user captive, Truth told, phones have become idols in the hands of so many, making it hard for users to be separated from them even when God is in the house. Sometimes it makes one a victim and at other times it makes the victim the culprit. Such is the strength of its power and hegemony. Idolatry can have no more succinct definition.

Designed to Cheat

The design of most modern mobile devices has become increasingly small, but their reach and disruptive capabilities appear to continue to double. In many ways we can say that the possibility to cheat with great dexterity and by users who themselves are very smart is designed into nearly all mobile phones. This is the reason the phones are referred to as "smart phones". They assume such a presence with their owners that any time one parts ways with them, the emptiness one feels is nearly akin to leaving one's own soul behind and the owner of the soul becomes very restless until the person reunites with it. They are often loved and cherished more than a person's most precious possession, and in the extreme cases missed above the most loved human relationship. Arguably, the screens of our mobile devices are stared at under an hour's time frame more than the faces of all persons we love and cherish in a month's period put together, and that includes persons we deem the closest in our lives. People simply cannot part ways with their smart phones and the so many other communication gadgets that are churned out at the Silicon Valley and other electronic incubators all across the world, depending on which one that outwits the others in the brutal fight for users' electronic soul.

Speaking ordinarily, it should be nobody's business what one does with one's smart devices. However, whenever its hold is so powerful that it comes in the way of personal commitment and communion with the creator and to the degree of disturbing the peaceful worship of other believers, then it is time to get worried. That has become the unfortunate testimony of many individuals. But the disabling effects of these devices are clearly not limited to crippling our spiritual disciplines. Their reach far extends to nearly every aspect of life that matters to their users. Their use has very proudly dwarfed most other things that an average person would normally engage with every day. But of a greater concern for this book is their effect on the corporate gatherings of God's people. Sometimes they constitute agents that perpetrate and perpetuate uncivil and inconsiderate behavior toward others. The problem in our hands is a situation where the use of a person's mobile device becomes one of the reasons why God's people can no longer worship him without undue interruptions. A situation where a person's lifestyle and convenience becomes a hindrance to the proper functioning of the body of Christ must be completely unacceptable. Thus, the task of resisting every such personal intrusion is one which calls for the attention of the entire body of Christ.

Perhaps we can ask, why use these gadgets during worship in the church? The reason could be that the church is the one place where things that are abhorrent and intolerable in the public square often happen with impunity. Most public institutions and organizations vehemently forbid the use of mobile devices within their premises. Most of them have taken far-reaching steps to enforce these prohibitions. Such institutions as the Law Courts, banks and other finance houses, movie theaters, airplanes, certain locations in educational institutions, military units and installations, hospital wards and operating theatres etc., have come out with extreme measures to deter the so-called 'inconsiderate phone users'. Violations in places such as the above usually attract sanctions and steps are taken to enforce the ban.

Churches however face a different kind of challenge in this area. Preventing the use of mobile devices during worship services has proven nearly impossible. Mere announcements and warning posters appear inadequate, prompting some churches in some parts of the world to seek other extreme measures such as installing telephone jammers to block transmissions, and by so doing denying worshipers' telephones access to their networks. However, the high cost of such equipment would not permit every church to take such extreme and expensive measures. It must be pointed out however, that despite such stringent measures, these inconsiderate phone users have rarely been successfully deterred. In the end, the task and responsibility of managing our social media devices rests on the individual worshiper. This to me is where the true test of obedience and loyalty lies.

Can you not watch with me for an hour?

Perhaps, the solution may well lie on a continuous appeal to individual Christians' consciences and obedience to church rules and regulations, as well as consideration for the wellbeing of others. Such appeal of course would involve for the most part illustrating with this incident involving Jesus our master and his disciples. At the peak and most painful period of Jesus' ministry on earth, he sought more closeness to a few of his disciples. During the days leading to his crucifixion, he went with three of them to the garden of Gethsemane. Having instructed them to wait at a particular location, he went a short distance further away from them to pray. After praying and having the famous "let this cup pass me by" dialogue with his father, he returns and finding them all sleeping. He asks Peter, (the one who ought to know better) in an apparent tone of surprise, "What! Could you not watch with me for an hour?" (Matthew 26:40). In other words, Jesus was asking them, 'could you not sacrifice a little sleep to feel with me what I feel? Would you not give up any comfort for the greater good? The disciples had a right to sleep but Jesus required them to stay awake and support him for just a short while. They failed.

I urge every reader of this book to think seriously and deeply about this incident. We must confront this same question today. Are we prepared in all honesty, to watch with Jesus for an hour or two without

Worshiping Disorders

idolizing our communication gadgets? Church Services and programs clearly don't go on for eternity. Much of every week belongs to the individual. In corporate gatherings or personal devotions, God demands but a tiny fraction of your time to fellowship with him. As a matter of fact, most worship services especially in the Western world are observably brief, at least when compared to worship services in much of African and other developing countries where spending long hours in worship services are regarded as a privilege rather than an encroachment into the precious time of the participants.

Yet many Christians seem to have great difficulty reserving the entirety of this tiny fragment of our time to God alone. People look at their watches with great impatience and on occasion, confront the church leadership with embarrassing accusations of slightly exceeding the closing time. Perhaps the rush to leave the service is due mainly to people's desire to be reunited with their communication gadgets. One wonders then if their impatience in the presence of God has something to do with a desire to reconnect with their electronic gadgets! This simply may not be far from the truth because even while the service is ongoing, some people are seen to be very noticeably receiving calls in whispers or texting messages. There are yet others who practically trip on those sitting on their way in their rush to go and receive an incoming call. Even after the services, some of those who accuse the leadership of exceeding the worship time do not necessarily rush off to go home or to go to work. Rather, they are seen sitting for many more minutes with faces bowed over their phones or simply hanging out with friends and family within and around the church premises taking photographs with these gadgets. These are all the hard realities of our day. It is therefore not clear whether Jesus would have seen anything different if he should choose to hang out with us physically like he did with the three disciples. He would surely confront us with the same question or even a more frustrating expression of disappointment.

The assertion that mobile devices constitute such a menace and terror in the worship gatherings of the church is an undeniable reality. But there is a question that must bug the minds of every Christian worshiper. Why is it impossible for a Christian to disable his or her mobile device for "an hour" in order to dedicate an undisturbed and uninterrupted worship to God but is able to do so at the work place? Most people know that in many work places, employees are not allowed the use of their telephones while at work and they rigidly and absolutely respect that law no matter the urgency. Why is it then so hard to sacrifice a time that God simply must not share with anyone else? Who is so important for a serious minded worshiper to want to call at the same time they are in church to call on God? Whose call is so important that a serious worshiper must respond to at such times when God too, is calling for his children's undivided attention? These questions must keep you thinking, dear reader!

Worshiping Disorders

Admittedly, phones and other mobile devices when used responsibly can be very useful instruments in the hands of a serious worshiper. The problem is that there is no way to know when they are good company or the opposite. They are designed to do several things. They can be used to do an audio recording of an entire or some segments of a service that the user finds particularly interesting. They serve as note pads in a world where long hand writing on paper had diminished significantly. They have Bible apps that enable the users to download nearly every version of the Bible for their use during services. One of the challenges that many pastors do face however, under the present technological dispensation is actually to be able to recognize and accept the fact that life is fast moving away from paper to gadgets, and from manual to digital. Consequently, the paper teaching and learning resource materials as we know it is fast becoming obsolete as production of such materials have significantly shifted from print to the screen. Once they realize this, then the next step would be to ensure a proper and profitable utilization of the new reality instead of kicking against their use. However, that does not eliminate the problem of our discussion because there is also no denying the fact that while using smart phones for the good purpose, people still tend to succumb to the temptation of taking a peek at the other diversionary activities that are also possible. The urge to peek into Facebook, WhatsApp. Twitter, Instagram, Snapchat and other social media apps, or to check e-mails and phone messages (SMS) always

Worshiping Disorders

remain a strong possibility.

Despite all the cautions, telephones do still ring out incessantly and quite disturbingly during services. More troubling is the fact that the users of these phones seem to have no control over when they ring. They ring during the songs and hymn singing; they ring during prayers; they ring during sermons; they ring during announcements; they ring during the scripture readings and they ring during moments of silent meditation and personal contrition. They also ring during the Holy Communion celebration, during memorial services, and they ring during baptismal services. Mobiles phones remain the one constant defiant challenge to the church. Irrespective of the point in time they ring, every incoming call in any of the untamed mobile phones often does indescribable damage to the worship space and mood of God's people. The hour of worship should be a solemn hour when nothing ought to interfere no matter what that is.

Troubling also is the nature of the varying ringtones produced by the different brands and designs of mobile phones. Advancement in technology means that the ring tone with which telephones have always been associated has largely disappeared or simply become one small choice of tones out of many. With modern technology, just about any and every type of recordable sound can be uploaded as a ring tone including a chuckle or the cry of a baby or the tumultuous noise of a football crowd. As I write, the ringtone of my mobile telephone is the title track of my latest audio music album. While this creative diversity is a welcome development, it also creates huge problems with regard to the going off of phone sounds during a church service. There is always the risk of very offensive sounds that are not supposed to be heard in the sanctuary going off at random thereby polluting the prevalent spiritual atmosphere. It would for example be highly embarrassing to hear Eminem's "Ass like that", or Michael Jackson's "I'm bad" or perhaps Justin Bieber's "Oh Girl!" and not to talk of Lady Gaga's "Cheek to cheek", and several other obscene and explicit song-turned ring tones interrupt proceedings during a service. Some of these songs can be so toxic that the introduction of any of them under a worship service would most certainly do unimaginable damage. The possibility of such happening must create real worry for church leaders whose duty it is to ensure that serious worshipers do worship in a quiet and conducive atmosphere.

Some Possible Deterrents

The task of combating the assault by mobile devices on Christian worship is the primary responsibility of the owners and users of the devices and that comes from a personal conscious fear of God and consideration for the right of other worshipers to worship in an atmosphere of undisturbed serenity. Church regulations and repeated announcements often fall on deaf ears for the most part and thus always unable to rein in violators. Church leaders consequently are quite often, left in a difficult situation not knowing what to do next. This therefore, puts the responsibility of compliant behavior with regards to the use of mobile devices in the house of God squarely on the owners, something that must be motivated mostly only, by a disciplined and civil disposition and respect for others. Self-discipline in this case must be able to accomplish what public rebuke is unable to. The reason, as earlier stated, is because while governments and organizations often take the most extreme measures to enforce their 'no phone' policies, the church for the most part appears very helpless and fiscally unable to take similar measures. Offenders understand full well that the church is under no mood to use the law-enforcement agencies or to institute legal proceedings against them. In many ways therefore, the church finds itself in the position of weakness, unfortunately not by reason of any attacks by enemies from without, but by reason of in-house acts of indiscipline. This is a very dangerous trend and a serious affront to the God of the church. Perhaps I will have to say this if it would help to deter some, take it or leave it, whenever a person deliberately elevates self above God, or intentionally holds God's people hostage, heaven may react swiftly and forcefully. Similarly, whenever a person intentionally hurts the church with a sense of avoidable impunity, the God of the church should not keep silent and accept it. The church isn't completely helpless. It might be helpful to illustrate this point with this incident in the bible.

In Acts of the Apostles chapter 12, we read how Herod the king began to enjoy the acts of harassing people from the young church. Once comfortable and unchallenged with his newfound game, he began the hobby of killing the few highly-placed pillars of the church. First, he picks up James the brother of John and slaughters him with the sword. Emboldened by the hilarious cheers of his Jewish fans he picks up Peter to give him the same treatment. However, strong Jewish religious tradition of Unleavened Bread, coupled with God's intervention on behalf of the young and vulnerable church set in motion events that put a break to the killings, and eventually set the stage for the tragic end of the 'troubler' of God's people. But more significantly, Herod's sad demise is to later serve to demonstrate the awesomeness of God's power over the lives of all brutes and 'troublers' of the church of Christ everywhere and every time. Readers must recall that by the time the curtain falls on his story, King Herod is utterly and shamefully wasted in the most agonizing manner while the church ran with tales of God' power and supremacy, and his ability to protect his very own as well as his glory. The bottom line is; those who deliberately come in the way of God's lifting by his children and his church will be stopped on their tracks and we may not know how God would choose to do so. This illustration may be viewed as severe but sometimes it is good to jolt us to the fact that the God of mercy and grace is also the same God of judgment lest we run with the understanding of only one aspect of God's nature in our dealings with him. The church will continue to march on and the gates of Hades cannot prevail against it. Social media platforms' assault is proving to be one of those gates and this shall also not prevail against the church's ability to worship the almighty God, undisturbed.

I can raise another question here to help us discuss this issue further. Should the battle against phone disturbances be viewed as both a physical and spiritual one? Is it only a battle of conscience, an appeal only to people's sense of reason? I submit that the problem must be tackled from all fronts. First, Church leadership must continue to make open appeals through the regular announcements both from the pulpit and through printed instruction on the worship bulletin and flyers in and around the church notice boards. Secondly, ushers and church officials should also politely signal to people who are spotted fiddling with their devices to kindly desist from doing so provided such appeal is made in a way that would not interfere with people's ability to concentrate and in the most civil way. Thirdly, prominence must be given to prayer in checkmating this problem. When people are invited to join in corporate prayers on an issue that the church is struggling with, they tend to understand their part in helping to find solutions better. Corporate prayer of repentance oftentimes is more than a thousand words of rebuke, instructions and announcements. Every concerned child of God must view modern technology as potential tools for success, but beyond that they must also view with seriousness, their potential as disruptive tools in the hands of a ferocious enemy who would stop at nothing to use every available instrument to inflict maximum damage to the worship of the Almighty God.

I will conclude this important chapter with a very pertinent warning by author Dawn who observes, "Indeed, advances in technology bring us many advantages, but the advantages are always coupled with profound losses-primarily the loss of community"[27] This loss is the inestimable loss of attention to worship proceedings, a loss of interaction with fellow worshipers, a loss of the powerful presence of God among his people and indeed a loss of virtually everything geared towards a proper worship of God. When a worshiper goes home with no story of God's visitation, attendance to the worship service amounts to a complete waste of time which is what our adversary the devil really goes all out to achieve.

The apostle Paul speaks about tearing down every "proud obstacle" that is raised against the knowledge of Christ (2Corinth. 10:5) As a matter of fact, no telephone must be allowed to ring while God's people are worshiping. Because the worship hour is often the time when God's children take a spiritual flight into

---

[27]Dawn, p. 27

Worshiping Disorders

God's presence, powered by the Holy Spirit, all communication gadgets ought invariably and compulsorily to be switched to the flight mode, or out rightly turned off or as many have learnt to do, totally put out of sight. Surely you can tarry with Jesus for a while. Choosing to do that must be applauded as a deliberate act of worship in itself when a person says to God; *I choose your presence above all other presences; I choose my conversation with you above all others; and I choose to offer you my ears and my heart above all else.* Every time you make such a decision, God is honored and he takes good notice. My friend, when God takes notice of you, you are in for the most wonderful time of your life and your value in his sight increases exponentially.

BUSY BODIES; BEDDED PEWS

Unwarranted loitering and restlessness among worship participants during worship services has remained one of the many struggles that many churches face. Some people simply like to loiter about while worship is in progress for reasons that most often they themselves are unable to explain. Sometimes, there is a sense that a certain unseen power keeps a person moving up and down and, in many cases, purposelessly. Where do people go during church services? Just what are they looking for outside of the sanctuary while service is progress? In many churches and in many places these busy bodies are never in short supply. This is very unhealthy behavior that church leadership is often too handicapped to tackle. People who display such attitudes quite often advance reasons to justify their actions. Part of the reason, as I pointed out earlier is that church is not the place to openly confront people, which is something that very many people understand all too well. The church is just about the one place of gathering where people's idiosyncrasies find unchallenged accommodation. When such undesirable idiosyncrasies are challenged at all, it most often takes the form of pacifism since church leaders are expected to be nice and forbidden from overtly embarrassing people.

Church is the one place where people smile while suffering. Ushers and church wardens struggle to put up smiling faces even when their entreaties to worship participants meet with snubs and the middle finger. Most people that behave in such uncultured and uncivil manners often forget that God, not people is the one being dishonored. They fail to heed the words of the Prophet Habakkuk who told God's people, "The Lord is in His holy temple: let all the earth keep silence before Him." (Habakkuk. 2:20.) Keeping silent before God simply as a demonstration of honor and reverence to him has increasingly become very difficult in our day. Restless behavior during worship services can be attributed to some factors. I will discuss a few of them that readily come to mind.

a. A lack of purpose: Concentration is nearly impossible when a person is in church for all the wrong reasons. Many people view church gatherings as providing them with the opportunity to 'catch up' with friends and acquaintances. Consequently, such people stand in corners, at the church corridors and car parking lots to discuss their businesses and other issues of mutual interest regardless of what goes on inside the sanctuary. While church gatherings obviously provide rare opportunities for worshipers to catch up and socialize, the timing of such an activity may however be wrong. Most churches often build in post-service socializing opportunities, often around tea and coffee tables (In Sweden it is called "Fika time"), thus enabling people to concentrate while the service lasts, with the knowledge that opportunities exist after service for catching up and socializing. However, this knowledge scarcely deters some people who are set in their ways and who simply can't wait patiently until that segment of the service thereby creating real hardship for church administrators and managers.

b. A lack of commitment to purpose: Understanding the purpose for attending a church service is one thing, giving a dedicated commitment to that purpose is another thing altogether. When a person fails to fully understand and commit to the purpose of going to church, it becomes very hard and nearly impossible to achieve and maintain concentration during service. The major reason Christians go to church is to worship God who they believe is present at every worship gathering. The second reason for gathering is for mutual fellowship and encouragement of one another. Scarcely do Christians gather together without purpose. Consequently, once a person does not have either of the above in mind, then it becomes difficult if not impossible for the person to pay attention to the proceedings or participate fully in the service. Thus it would not be surprising to see people in this category display disturbing conducts during the service. The first visible symptom of this is that such a person becomes impatient and restless, causing movements and conducts that in the end become uncomfortable and disturbing to others.

Worshiping Disorders

One obvious casualty of a lack of commitment to purpose, beyond the harm it does to the general atmosphere in the church is that the culprit loses the will to join in the rituals of the worship liturgical acts. Personal convenience takes over the collective good. Worshiping God in the real sense of the word is not always convenient. It is never convenient to go through the rituals of anything at all, which is the reason praise is referred to in the Holy Bible as a "sacrifice" (Hebrews 13:15). It takes purpose and dedication to the Christian calling to really commit to bringing joy and pleasure to the God that Christians serve. When these are lacking, the possibility for a person being an active participant in the midst of worshipers becomes very obviously diminished.

c. A lack of preparedness: This point is slightly linked to the problem of punctuality to church. A lack of preparedness and anticipation has repercussions on a person's ability to have a feeling of settlement and concentration during a worship service. This is because getting to church in good time enables one to sort out some of the very personal issues that often bring about restless conditions and unnecessary movements once service is underway. For example, such things as unplanned last ditch visits to the rest room, emptying one's coat of personal items and hanging the same at the cloak room, getting a drink of water or changing shoes as often happens with many during the messy days of winter, all often demand consideration in terms of time. In addition, in many churches, finding available car-parking spaces often presents a challenge thereby, occasioning late entrance to the sanctuary despite early arrival to the church premises. Also, nursing parents or parents of toddlers often underestimate the level of challenges their children can pose. Consequently, panic movements are necessitated when these toddlers need one form of attention or the other in the middle of the service. Readying the necessary nursery materials and sitting at locations that make for a quick and easy exit from the sanctuary would certainly help to prevent unnecessary disturbances.

d. Disregard and incivility toward other worshipers: We are enjoined as Christians to be our brothers' keepers and also to treat others as we want to be treated. This is the core of civility which should rule the world. We believe that the church is a beacon, a light set on the hill for everyone to see, an epitome of civil behavior and love. The church should attract people not repulse them; the church should embrace people not dismiss them; the church should lead the way in orderliness not chaos. So the Church is not just a holy place, it is also a public space where due consideration ought to be given to the comfort of all other participants. Some worship attendees do things that impede the ability of others to concentrate, showing little or no regard for how people sitting around them feel or are affected. This point is so vitally important that it would require much attention the reason being that church is one place where people go to find the one thing that is impossible to find elsewhere which is a spiritual sanctuary and a connection with God and other like-minded people. It is the place where the sorrowful come to find joy; where the bereaved come for comfort and spiritual support and, it is the one place where the hungry soul come for the bread that cannot be baked with hands. Indeed, the church is the 'wailing wall' for very many Christians. During times of natural disasters or conflict, the church also becomes the 'shelter in times of storm' for Christians and non Christians alike. Consequently, every visitor to the church ought to be very much aware of the right of others to be able to find a convenient space for whatever reason that brings them there.

Many do come to church with the utmost degree of serious mindedness and anticipation. When they come only to discover that the peace and tranquility that is often taken for granted in the house of God is far-fetched due to the activities of other people, they often become very discouraged. Some people, through their conducts and idiosyncrasies hold other genuine worshipers to ransom or even drive some away.

To further emphasize this point, I will discuss two categories of issues. The first category refers to those things that are often beyond a person's control while the second includes those things that are very avoidable through commitment to self-discipline. For example, parents might not contribute to the restless attitudes of some children at church who oftentimes keep their parents on their toes, causing distractions

Worshiping Disorders

that have consequences on the orderly atmosphere within the sanctuary. Similarly, we often might not make decisions about when nature calls us to visit the rest rooms thereby triggering occasional movements; nor do we determine just those rare moments when the bad air makes its escape from a bad or constipated stomach! On the other hand however, there are things that are completely within our own decision to do or not to do. For example persistent and purposeless movements during worship, side-talks and gesticulations that disturb and distract others, sounds of social media notifications and pop ups, constant feet-shuffling, feet stomping (when we are not dancing in praise and worship), or placing legs on occupied or unoccupied chairs, gum-chewing especially in such manners that produce pops and sounds, crinkling of candy wrappers and other noisy papers and objects, or carrying a child that does the same, or even when spouses are unable to refrain from romantic cuddles that run contrary to spiritual context or atmosphere are all within our ability to control and refrain from. In addition, when sometimes babies and infants cry, snort or play in nauseating manners, parents often hesitate to live up to expectations to put the situation under control. Most often parents hesitate to carry the restless infants off to the nursery rooms and attend to them accordingly. They appear oblivious of just how disruptive the children's activities can be to those sitting nearby. Sometimes also, it can be very disruptive when toddlers are left to run uncontrollably around the sanctuary especially when such movements can be controlled or minimized.. Sometimes too, the very active ones are seen grabbing the microphones or going to felicitate with the singers or even the preacher, to the admiration of the grinning and nodding parents but often to the disapproval of other worshipers. Unfortunately however, parents of those children usually show signs of agitation and sometimes out right aggressive looks should other people intervene to stop their children's disruptive activities.

To a large degree, there is a certain unspoken assumption by parents that everyone ought to show tolerance or admiration to their children's' disruptive behavior since they are also the children of the church. Unfortunately, very many serious-minded participants often do not accede to such assumptions, reason being among other things, that those who do not as yet have much or any experience with toddlers are most likely to view such conducts as completely unacceptable. Moreover, some parents are still able to bring their own children under control and they do not understand why others would not do the same! Whatever the case and no matter who is concerned, no one that goes to the house of God for worship has any readiness to put up with conducts capable of disrupting the desired purpose.

Perhaps parents can take a cue on child discipline in Christian gatherings by a story recorded in that great parenting book titled *Dare to Discipline* (198, 2018) by

Worshiping Disorders

James Dobson. Dobson himself recalled one time when he was ministering and from the stage, saw his young children tumbling upside down on their seats in the pews. He came down from the stage and everyone watched as he quietly went to his kids, turned their heads and placed their buttocks on their seats probably with a firm reprimand to behave themselves! Thereafter, he returned to the pulpit and resumed his ministration! I guess he needed to practice what he wrote about and not give his children an opportunity to manipulate him at that time. After all, to their small minds, daddy was far away and busy so we can play. Now tell me, do you think those kids were shocked and did they learn the lesson that rules will be enforced no matter the place, the time and the people watching? What about the parents and other kids who witnessed this demonstration of disciplinary action? Don't you think it will strengthen their resolve to act that way and also warn those who would excuse such behavior that it isn't acceptable? Other kids who throw tantrums will also learn that they can be reined in even in public. I bet that he would have followed up with talks and discussions with the kids after service to further entrench the need for orderly behavior in church and other public places in their minds! Why don't we let our children run around inside airplanes no matter how petulant they become? The obvious reason is that there are rules for our safety and they are enforced!

To further illustrate how irksome this issue can be, an article by the Forerunner titled "Proper Sabbath-

Worshiping Disorders

Service Behavior", also observes,

> "It is unfortunate that complaints about inappropriate behavior at church services are so common. Whether it is boisterous children, giggling and note-passing teenagers, a too-affectionate couple, someone constantly going in and out of the hall or a snoring "listener," poor church behavior is distracting and disrespectful. No group—big or small, in a rented hall or a member's home—seems to be immune to this persistent problem."

"Not one of us" it continues, "wants to attend a church in which anarchy reigns!"[28] It means then that responsibility rests on each and every worshiper, parents and all others concerned, to ensure that through decent and spirit-controlled behavior, every attitude capable of causing anarchy in the house of God is decidedly avoided at all costs. Some people may argue though, whether any type of behavior is indeed capable of impeding or distracting a serious-minded worshiper. To that I would say that much depends on individuals and their capacity to handle distraction. But at least few people would doubt the fact that distraction in any sphere of activity-be it at the work space, research space laboratory space or public library is always an unwelcomed phenomenon

---

[28]Forerunner "Proper Sabbath-Service Behavior"

Worshiping Disorders

and the severest steps are often taken to prevent them. Issues relating to disturbances are however, not to be viewed only in terms of disturbing public peace, especially when it relates to church services. God enjoins us to maintain orderliness.

Church services are holy appointments between a holy God and his children in diverse places whom he has made holy and set apart for mutual communion on certain days and times of each week. Christians do not simply gather; they gather on invitation and for definable purposes. The following scriptures say as much. In 1John 1:3, the apostle declares, "… that ye also have fellowship with us: and truly our fellowship is with the Father, and with His son Jesus Christ." Genesis 49:10 says that much, "…and unto him *shall the gathering of the people be.*" Also in Matthew 18:20, God promises that "…where two or three are gathered together in (My) name, there am I in the midst of them". So important is the day of worship in Isaiah 58:13 that God calls it, "My holy day Consequently, the ability of God's people to have this holy gathering successfully and in tranquility must be deemed as an honor given to the God who is the chief convener of every such gathering.

e. Discourteous and Uncivil Behavior to Ushers and Church Officials: I must also make mention of yet one more troubling behavior namely, the prevalent issue of disrespect and disregard for church officials who are saddled with the task of ensuring that order prevails in the church. It is common knowledge that one group whose temperaments are frequently put to constant test is the ushers and greeters group whose task it is to receive and usher parishioners to the pews. In many cases, these men and women have been recipients of cold shoulders and snobbish treatments by worship participants who appear to question the ushers' authority to deny them their preferred sitting positions, or wonder why the ushers have to touch the shoulders of slumbering worshipers in an attempt to have them stay alert. These church workers often have to endure some uncomplimentary remarks from the very same people they are there to serve. Worshipers who display such dispositions often go totally against all civility in their behavior, and unnecessarily make the task of those who volunteer to maintain order in the house of God extremely difficult. One of the reasons worshipers do this is because ushers and greeters do not have 'policing' powers, nor do they ever pretend to have the authority to forcefully deter anyone in church who engages in any disturbing act. The only authority they possess, if any, is such as the entire congregation confers on them; to maintain order and the right atmosphere in the service. Consequently, it is really very hard for them to succeed in a situation where the worshipers fail to cooperate with them. Whenever the people cooperate and there is order, everything goes well. When that is the case, joy and fellowship fills the air and the Lord is happy with his children. When the opposite is the case however, anarchy follows and the peaceful atmosphere in the sanctuary gets disrupted.

Worshiping Disorders

The apostle Paul charges in "1Corinthians 14:40, "Let all things be done decently and in order." The right of everyone who leaves home to go to a worship service to worship in an atmosphere of undisturbed and uninterrupted peace and orderliness must be guaranteed and respected to the fullest. To do that requires the unflinching cooperation of every worshiper with those people charged with the task of maintaining order during the service.

Thinking generally about this issue of restless people at church reminds me of the fourth Commandment in Exodus 20 which says, "Remember the Sabbath day, to keep it holy." In the commandment, certain vital elements are often ignored in search of the bigger picture. The major responsibilities do not often lie in avoiding work and other vital chores on the "Sabbath day" depending on which day is "Sabbath" for each congregation and each individual. Those responsibilities are often hidden amidst the end result of a person's behavior and conduct in whatever they do on the day in question of which the worship gathering is a significant part. Thus, character, respect and consideration for the comfort and wellbeing of people whose purpose and desire is genuinely honoring God in worship in his own temple must get prime position in whatever way the above commandment is interpreted.

Bedded Pews

On the direct opposite side of restless worshipers are

those who can barely stay awake through the service due to struggle with sleep and weariness. This category of people is hereby referred to as the "Bedded Pew" in this section due to the often uncomfortable sights of worshipers slouching on church pews during services. Sights of people overcome by tiredness and sleep during church services are common spectacles in many church gatherings. But few people if any at all attend services with the intention to sleep or display obvious tiredness because dozing off or sleeping in church can very embarrassing and a waste of precious time for a person who has come all the way to attend.

Tired and sleeping worshipers are not helpful in a church service for a number of reasons. First, they often constitute a nightmare to the ushers whose task it is to ensure physical alertness and active participation by everyone present. Secondly, sleepers create lots of attention and often constitute a distraction and disturbance to those sitting next to or around them. There is a third reason however, one found in the bible why sleeping during worship is inappropriate and sometimes can attract some degree of negative consequence.

In Acts 20:7-12, what seemed to be a somewhat funny incident took place in the city of Troas where on the first day of the week, as this story goes, the disciples had gathered to break bread. Paul, knowing that he would depart from the city spoke to the people in an upper room illuminated with lamps until midnight. A young man named Eutychus sitting by the window was "sinking into a deep sleep" while Paul preached to the people. When he was overcome with sleep he fell three floors to the ground and died instantly. However, his case ended on a miraculous note as the Lord raised him up through the timely intervention of the Apostle Paul. I believe that this incident was so noteworthy that it was recorded in the canon of Scripture for posterity to see what can go really wrong when people turn meeting places into sleeping chambers. Fortunately, Eutychus lived to tell his story, but sometimes not everyone can be that fortunate. While miracles still clearly happen, readers must however be warned that there are not many Saint 'Pauls' in our day, at the same time that church buildings have become much higher than three 'storeys' and decked with far greater capacities for comfort and relaxation.

In short, the atmospheric conditions in many churches today can at best be described as directly sleep-inducing thereby raising a much higher risk for more comfort and a lull to sleep than that at Paul's meeting. But in our day too things have improved beyond what they had, and chances of a fall are at the barest minimum. But where that happens as a result of sheer accident, death may not necessarily result. However, cases where people have been known to fall off the pews when overcome by tardiness are not uncommon. There is also the fact that slumbering or sleeping amidst other worshipers more often than not causes untold embarrassment for the sleeper. Nothing can be more embarrassing than those audible snores and sometimes with gushing saliva, which inescapably attract attention and leaving other worshipers struggling to tolerate such display. In fact, just about everything that makes for self-embarrassment can take place when once a person slips into partial unconsciousness, surrendering to the untimely call of nature in a public space. Such people often immediately become a spectacle, an embarrassing cynosure of all eyes with children sometimes watching in great delight and making fun of them. They do not make the pews richer. They make the pews poorer; poorer to behold, like when you view one sickly fruit in a bunch of other healthy fruits on a tree branch, hanging weakly, color changed, and about to fall prematurely. No one should truly aspire for this type of identity.

Indeed, sleeping during church service or public gatherings has throughout the ages been a recurring experience for many but it is one habit that appears to gather momentum as life presents greater challenges that often expose people to heightened stress and anxiety. Some writers have tried to identify some factors responsible for sleeping or slumbering at meetings. David Padfield was one of those. In his article titled, 'Sleeping Saints', he points to something he refers to as "The Late Show" in which he points fingers at people who stay up Saturday night to watch the late show. Such people he says usually cannot keep their eyes open on Sunday morning. The main problem with them he points out; is one of" priorities". Once people fail to prioritize schedules considered of vital importance to them, important areas of their lives are bound to suffer. He goes on to observe,

"Those who stay up Saturday night to watch the late show usually can't keep their eyes open on Sunday morning. Their problem is one of priorities. The gospel of Christ rates well below reruns of World War II movies and the latest slasher films."[29] People like that often underestimate the limitations of the human body. The result is that staying up late on a Saturday whether it be as a result of work or leisure, will unquestionably affect physical, mental and spiritual alertness on a Sunday morning. Consequently, caution must be exercised to know when it is time to simply shut down and retire to bed. Another helpful tip would therefore be to avoid non-scheduled and non-essential duties; especially those that fall within a person's choice as much as possible. This is especially necessary for those who are active functionaries in the worship service such as choristers, ushers, Scripture readers, Sunday school teachers, prayer leaders and Pastors etc. If possible at all, only dire and completely unavoidable circumstances should be the reason for not getting sufficient rest on the eve of a scheduled worship service.

Some additional factors have been identified and associated with sleeping during services. These factors

---

[29] David Padfield, "Sleeping Saints"

include among others:

a. A Lack of interest: Padfield identifies "lack of interest" as one of the reasons individuals are overcome with sleep during church services and other meetings. According to him, "…if someone were to lecture on how to make a million dollars in real estate, these folks would find a way to stay awake, even if they had to put toothpicks in their eyelids to keep them open."[30] This observation obviously brings into focus a person's real interest and motivation for attending a church event. Real interest generates mental and spiritual alertness which inevitably sustains physical alertness. In any venture where a person holds a stake, boredom and tiredness are often resisted with the greatest possible determination. But detached participation and lack of personal interest has little or no resistance to any opposing challenge at all, be it physical or emotional. However, church is not for personal gain as much as it is about worshiping our common Lord. Put in another way, it is not about us at all. It is about him, and those who sincerely desire to worship him are very often motivated to resist all principalities in order to be able to do so. Succumbing to the forces of nature may just be one clear indication of a clear lack of interest in the corporate worship of God's people. However, in the spirit of our Christian calling and our standing compulsion to extend common civility to others, those who are stronger must be tender-hearted

---

[30] Ibid

towards those who are weak, while those who are weak must take practical steps to get over or mitigate their weakness.

b. Working the Midnight Shift: Padfield also identified something he called "Working The Midnight Shift". There are those whose work schedules necessitate a regular surrender of their weekend nights. We identify two different groups here. On the one side are those who by the nature of their work have no influence over their weekend schedule. People on very essential duties such as security workers, health sector workers, media personnel, transport sector workers, etc, often fall within this category. Such people out of necessity work through the night and only return in time enough to prepare and leave for church. In fairness to people in this category, one must acknowledge that they indeed show great determination worthy of commendation. It is both a strong act of faith and boldness for such persons to insist on attending church rather than staying home to have their well-deserved sleep. People like that are often confronted with a huge dilemma. Their love for God and their unwillingness to abstain from corporate worship would not let them stay back from a worship service. On the other hand, attending church and sleeping through the entire service with the added risk of disturbing other worshipers thereby portraying the church in a bad light especially to visitors obviously makes the matter a choice between the rock and the hard place. This group of people actually appreciate that ushers tap them awake whenever their heads lull in sleep.

But there is a second category of potential church sleepers. This category is made up of people who often, avoidably take on extra job schedules on Saturday nights apparently in order to boost their income capacity. People who do such, arguably, intentionally set themselves up for either missing church on Sunday or come knowing with a high degree of certainty that staying alert through the service would be almost impossible. Sometimes one wonders whether such behavior is not tantamount to offering God only a person's residual time. If not, church ought to be factored into a person's weekly schedule, even if a certain degree of sacrifice by way of reduced weekly earnings has to be made. That takes great trust in God's capacity to provide to even give such an option a single thought.

In any case, whatever the reason for keeping late nights on the eve of Sunday worship might be, staying alert through the service will invariably be a huge challenge. Understandably, some people are more resilient than others and can withstand the challenges presented by tired bodies. It should be up to each individual therefore, who is serious about attending worship services to evaluate their capacities. Failure to do so would invariably continue to fill the pews of churches with tired and sleepy body presences, something which does not bode well for the integrity and healthy function of Christian worship.

c. Medication: Worship participants who have a medication regimen easily make it to the list of Church Sleepers. Some medications invariably weaken the nerves thereby inducing drowsiness and sleep. This usually creates a dilemma for those involved as they are faced with the choice of staying away from church services or risking the obvious consequences posed by the medications. Napping during the service is the immediate possible consequence of that and the persons involved may have little or no resistance at all. This raises the question as to what the approach of church leaders towards this vulnerable group should be. Looking at it properly, a convenient solution to this type of problem may be far-fetched. However, a good first step must be to ensure people struggling with this challenge do not suffer any form of embarrassment from church officials. It may be very helpful for church officials to familiarize themselves with the affected worship participants in order to ensure that they get all the needed support. When persons who are dependent or vulnerable due to conditions beyond their control dare to defy their challenges and make it to God's presence, God most certainly understands and accommodates them the way they are. God honors their faith more than their action or inaction.

The prophet Isaiah captures God's preparedness to accommodate the weak in chapter 40:11 of his prophecy, "He will feed his flock like a shepherd. He will carry the lambs in his arms, holding them close to his heart. He will gently lead the mother sheep with their young." [NLT] God cares for the strong as well as the weak. He never seeks to embarrass those who do not run as fast as the others and so should the church not do too. We should always be ready to accommodate those that God accommodates. Rather than repudiate or ignore the sick and vulnerable that came around him, Jesus constantly cared for them, healing and sending many home, completely remade. The church must always strive to adopt the same attitude towards the weak ones among us.

What then should be the responsibility of those disposed to falling asleep as a result of the issues I have discussed especially those who are under medication? One smart way would be to ensure that they occupy pews comfortable enough to protect them from potential slips or falls on those sitting close to them. They should also not sit in prominent locations in the church where everyone will be witnessing their struggles which they themselves may be oblivious of. For example, it would be inappropriate for them to be made to sit in the front areas of the church where they will be exposed to ridicule due to their snores and other potentially embarrassing behavior. In addition, it would be similarly inappropriate to allow personal vulnerabilities to disrupt the attention of entire fellow congregants who themselves might be completely unprepared for other people's personal struggles. Consequently, it should be the task of church officials to work with people in this category to figure out the best ways to assist them that would be both sympathetic and considerate to other worship participants.

d. Sunday Morning Hangovers: People often tend to underestimate the effects on the human body of long weekends of social activities and night outs. Saturday nights are particularly very tempting as it often forms the bedrock of all manner of engagements that result in people retiring late with the obvious consequence of getting insufficient sleep and strength required to stay active during the ensuing worship services the morning after. Thus it can be said that the fallout of Saturday nights are immediate and visible on Sunday mornings. Without at all implying that the children of God should refrain from such important socializing potentials that the weekends provide, what is important however, is to be fully aware that every true Christian has a common ecclesiastical duty a couple of hours down the line. Hebrews 10:25a reminds us about "not forsaking our own assembling together, as is the habit of some" (NASB). It means that Christian fellowship of which Sunday services around the world is very primal is a sacred call for all God's people and must never be sacrificed on the altar of social activities. Staying up late at night for whatever reasons contributes to sleep deprivations whose effects impede physical, mental and spiritual alertness and once that happens, nearly a whole congregation suffers the consequences as yet one more important participant in the holy assembly is left behind.

One obvious smart way to prevent getting caught up

with the hangovers of Saturday nights is to be mindful of a couple of things. First is to realize that your compatriots may not have the same communal church obligation as you do. As a devotee of the Christian faith, and a child of God, your 'Sundays' do not entirely belong to you. But for your compatriots who are probably either not Christians at all, or who do not take their Christian calling seriously, theirs belongs to them. Thus a sacred duty awaits you while none awaits them. Consequently, be alert to the temptations of peer pressure. Secondly, most social events, especially when they are not Christian in nature are very often awash with liquors and beverages that appear innocent at face value. When these are matched with 'good' friends that pressure you to "just taste a little", you may soon unwittingly fall victim of nerve-stimulating substances that would further endanger your ability to recover your agility on Sunday morning. Christians should never let down their guards irrespective of the environment and circumstance. James 4:7b cautions, "Resist the devil, and he will flee from you". There is an old music to the effect that "everybody likes Saturday nights". For those to whom their faith in Christ is a defining factor, Sunday morning holds not just more likes, but also more loves; love for the giver of life with whom every opportunity for fellowship is also a decisive defining moment of immense blessings and love for the brethren.

There is indeed no telling just how much of a problem sleeping under church services can generate for all concerned; the sleeper, the church leadership and the other participants as well. It is a practice that does no church any good. This habit can also, and indeed in some cases has been identified as a great source of discouragement to many pastors who begin to wonder whether there are things they are not doing right. Some go as far as to engage in self-indictment by assuming that the reason people sleep is because their sermons and other worship activities are boring and uninspiring. As laughable and often unrealistic as the thought or suggestion may sound dysfunctional worship church environment remain a concern for many ministers especially those among them who struggle with low self esteem and lack of self confidence. Such is the nature of the hydra-headed consequences of sleeping in church, a thing which worshipers must ask for the grace and wisdom to overcome.

Worshiping Disorders

"DRESSING FOR CHURCH"

Postmodern sensibilities have gradually encroached into the realm of dressing up for worship services. The church is now suffering from the 'everything casual' mentality of the 21st Century which sees multi billionaire CEO's address International business conferences on T-shirts and jeans trousers rather than the hitherto double-breasted corporate suits with matching ties. Such icons are increasingly becoming acceptable models of modern attire in public appearances. The late Rev. John DeBonville was so irked by the fact that this type of attitude is fast influencing people's attitude towards dressing for church that in an interview he once granted to CNN he was quoted as saying concerning such people,

"They saunter into church in baggy shorts, flip-flop sandals, tennis shoes and grubby T-shirts. Some even slide into the pews carrying coffee in plastic foam containers as if they're going to Starbucks. "It's like some people decided to stop mowing the lawn and then decided to come to church,"[31]

The vast majority of Christian worshipers do not seem to give the slightest attention any longer to what they wear to church. It appears that such aspects of their lives are no-go areas when it comes to living lives completely dependent on God's direction. After all,

---
[31] John De Bonville, "Stop Dressing So Tacky For Church"

what's God got to with it?

Questions surrounding how Christians ought to dress to church services have often not been as simple and obvious as they seem. This is because different Christian groups and denominations have opposing ideas regarding this aspect of life. In many cases, Christian costume debates get so heated up that it becomes a determinant factor for who's in and who's out. Some have inadvertently elevated the matter almost to doctrinal proportions whereby particular patterns of dressing for men and women respectively, are prescribed and rigidly adhered to with sometimes often embarrassing sanctions meted out to offenders. But this type of scenario very often comes with some consequences for a section of people. For example, visitors to such church groups who are oblivious of such dress regimes often emerge from meetings with tales of embarrassment. Also, those who have no desire to be concerned with such trivialities as dressing prescriptions are most likely to get very exasperated and discouraged. To avoid being drawn into such concerns, many worshipers especially the younger generation decide that keeping dressing as simple as possible is the best way to be 'cool' before God. Unfortunately, this 'coolness' in the end significantly plays into the hands of the spirit of the postmodern age the result of which becomes very obvious on the church pews.

Where then do we place the issue of dress code with regard to the concerns of this book namely, to address to the very core, dressings habits which are capable of negatively affecting our ability to worship in ways that are both acceptable and pleasing to God as well as respectful and considerate of other worshipers? Put in another way, how does physical appearance constitute a worshiping disorder? Does God really care? Do we have any biblical support to discuss how people physically appear before God during worship?

Arguably, outward appearance ought not to, under any circumstance whatsoever, constitute a hindrance to spiritual acts of worship, except of course when it gets to the point of constituting a distraction and conveying negative impressions about God's people. Once that becomes the case, physical appearance begins to attract some concerns. Sometimes what people wear can become a problem if it begins to fall out of tune with the values of the group to which the person belongs. There is a popular saying to the effect that the way you dress determines how you are addressed. By all standards therefore, the issues of dressing for church is one which must be properly addressed because it has implications for the way the church is viewed outside. But more importantly, it reveals something about people's willingness to be respectful to the sensibilities of the church who ought to model decency and decorum, and also to God before who everyone appears. But church aside, dressing is something taken very seriously in every occasion and in every culture and profession. There are both biblical and commonsense reasons to care about how we physically appear before God.

Worshiping Disorders

God is not just a lover of beauty and decency, God is the very definition of beauty. Late Christian singer Keith Greene in his brief musical career wrote a song which he titled, "O Lord, you're beautiful", a song dedicated to highlighting the beauty and splendor of God. Also, the Prophet Isaiah is quoted as saying, "Your eyes will see the King in His beauty" (Isaiah 33:17). In Psalm 27:4, King David, the Psalmist prayed to "Behold the beauty of the Lord". These individuals were well aware of not just the spiritual reality but also, the physicality of the one who made humans beautiful. Besides, only a beautiful God could have produced the beauty that we all see in his creation. Knowing all these, any suggestion that God would be uninterested in how his children look when they appear in his presence would be a gross misrepresentation of all reasonableness.

That idea of God's beauty is a truth which has a prominent place all through the Bible, something evidenced through simply looking at the human person which he created in his own likeness. It seems reasonable then that believers should appear reasonably beautiful and decently clad upon appearing before him. His own sense of beauty is widely known to be described in superlative terms and conspicuously displayed throughout creation. As a matter of fact, Scriptures record that "Splendor and majesty" are before God, (Psalm 96:6a). Consequently, in addition to good and decent appearance, there is an expectation that God's people more than any other community should add something of grace and dignity in their appearance. This is something that God would take great pleasure in because there ought to be a reflection of his attributes, a direct mirroring of he is in his children everywhere.

Unfortunately however, it is not always so among the generality of Christian worshipers and many seemingly have their own ideas and personal justifications for appearing the way they do, even if such considerations are in utter disregard for general decency. People like those have often taken the words of 1Samuel 16: 7 out of context to erroneously imply that God does not care about external appearances. In that text the Lord said to Samuel, "…for the Lord does not see as man sees; for man looks on the outward appearance, but the Lord looks on the heart." Once a text such as this is understood out of context, people often apply them to areas of life where they do not necessarily belong. In other words, they wrongly find in them a justification for the life style or in this case dress style they had always wanted.

God's purpose for Dressing: In ancient times, dressing or vestments, was always part of the preparation for worship. The priests wore garments fit for the various occasions for which they were tasked. In other words, different garments represented different moods and events. Joyful, solemn and sad times were all reflected in the patterns and colors of their attire. We will take a brief look at a few examples.

In Exodus 28:1-4 we read:

> And draw near to yourself Aaron your brother, and his sons with him, from among the children of Israel, that he may minister to me in the priest's office; Aaron, Nadav, and Abihu, Elazar, and Itamar, the sons of Aaron. And you shall make sacred garments for Aaron your brother, for honor and for beauty. And you shall speak to all who are wise hearted, whom I have filled with the spirit of wisdom, that they may make Aaron's garments to consecrate him that he may minister to me in the priest's office. And these are the garments which they shall make: a breastplate, and an ephod, and a robe, and a quilted undercoat, a mitre, and a girdle; and they shall make holy garments for Aaron your brother, and his sons, that he may minister to me in the priest's office...."

As we can see from the above text, God gave a sort of to-the-point prescription of what Aaron's priestly garment should be, and the designers of this garment had to be people who are 'wise hearted and filled with spirit of wisdom'. God's strong sense of fashion is powerfully revealed in this precise specification. Here God is seen as one who has a special particularity for great beauty, dignity and detail. This account is just one out of many such accounts in the Scriptures where God made demands for detailed specifications for beauty. Even in our day, many church traditions have retained the practice of prescribing certain dress codes for their priests, something which, as we can see dates back to Bible times and continuing throughout the ministries of the first Christians.

In another example, when God dressed Adam and Eve following their fall that introduced a previously non-existent feeling of shame, he was very particular concerning beauty and decency. Judging by the fashion trends at the time, Adam and Even couldn't have been dressed in any better way than they were. In providing clothing for both, two things may have been of utmost concern to God. First, God was concerned with covering their nakedness for purposes of decency which was brought about by their new sinful reality. Secondly, he was concerned about preserving their sense of dignity since he still cared very much about their wellbeing. As a result, the tunics of skin he clothed them not only covered of their nakedness but was also only more beautiful than the mere fig branches they ashamedly made for Think about this; the tunic was made by God's own hands and for that reason must have been the best clothing ever! (Genesis 3:21). This means then that God's purpose in human dressing is to maintain a sense of decent covering for humans as well as fostering a mentality of self-respect and dignity. Be that as it may, this book does not by any means., prescribe any pattern of dressing to anyone It is important to know that Christians have no prescribed uniforms in the sense in which schools and some public service institutions do. Nevertheless, there are a couple of values that Christian worshipers ought to bear in mind when considering what to wear to church activities and other social gatherings.

First, when we dress for church, decency, beauty and consideration for public scrutiny must be central in our mind. We simply must avoid clothes that promote indecent exposure on all occasions particularly during worship events. We can assume that just as God clothed Adam and Eve he still clothes his children today no make-up artist surpasses his sense of beauty and decency in that regard. In his Sermon on the Mount Jesus asked the crowd why they worried about clothing. Using the metaphor of the lilies of the field which neither toil nor spin yet they grow, he maintained that not even the super rich King Solomon was more beautiful than one of the lilies. The question that followed was very significant and relevant to our discussion here. He asked them, "If that is how God clothes the grass of the field, which is here today and tomorrow is thrown into the fire, will he not much more clothe you…." (Matthew 6:28-30). If God has vested interest in clothing us, why would we not then appear before him looking more beautiful than the lilies of the fields? Every child of God must strive to see that whatever God shows real and consistent interest in must also attract our interest else we will not be real children of our father.

A Man Is What He Wears: Perhaps, some readers would recognize the expression, "A man is what he wears". By extension, we should also say that "A woman is what she wears." In today's world, dressing often speaks louder than voice. It makes a statement about you even before you introduce yourself. Arguably, dressing is the first testimony to a person's status and identity, real or imagined. For example, bankers and people who work in other corporate establishments are often easily identifiable by their complete suit and ties while mechanics, engineers and factory workers are generally associated with multi-pocket overalls and helmets. In many third world cultures, a widow or widower mourning a spouse has a peculiar manner of dressing that makes them easily identifiable to sympathizers. In some African countries for example widows and widowers often wear white or complete black raiment that speak to their predicament for a period of time. Stephanie Paulsell in her book, *Honoring the Body* (2002) mentions this particular aspect. She observes, "Those in mourning often wear black, allowing their clothes to speak their grief to the world."[32]

But aside from mourners, people associated with certain gangs and peer groups are easily identifiable by their sagging pants and oversized T-shirts. In Sweden where this author resides, when one sees several folks dressed in black, then you suspect that they have been to a funeral service or surprisingly, a wedding. Also,

---

[32] Stephanie Paulsell, "Honoring the Body" p.60

the display windows in shopping malls in many countries announce the next high season on the horizon. When you see things that are scary, ghostly and bizarre for example, you know that 'Halloween' is around the corner. Similarly, when you see hearts and pink dresses beautifully displayed on shop windows, they most certainly announce to you that 'The Valentine's Day' is approaching. Christmas is announced by red or white clothes, or a combination of both, while Santa Lucia season is announced by white tube-like gowns and candle crowns. Furthermore, when people send out invitations for their birthdays and other parties, many of them generally prescribe the dress code expected of their guests ranging from pyjamas to three-piece suits. Guests are quite often expected to adhere strictly to such dress requirements or in some cases, simply abstain if they are unable to meet the conditions.

In almost all countries in the world also, Military personnel often wear special colorful outfits during celebratory parades and other special occasions from what they would wear if they were going for war. Children in most countries wear approved school uniforms to school, well laundered and often with distinguishing features and insignias. Those who dare to violate this requirement by wearing something else are often turned back or punished. What more can we say about the exquisite raiment of brides and grooms on the day of their wedding! Their unmatchable and glorious dressing often announces that indeed a day quite unlike no other in their lives had come. So special is such a day that proper arrangements are often made to ensure that exotic pictures are taken and hung at strategic positions in their home as a daily remembrance of their special day. Similarly, special robes, hats and hoods announce that new or graduating students are having their day in college institutions. All celebrity awards including the Oscars, Grammy, Bafta or BET often trigger a competition of sorts, for the best dressed. The Nobel Prize Awards ceremonies are often a showcasing of the best attires in the world.

Going further, it is evident that an invitation to the White House or Swedish Slott (Royal Palace) or other such places of importance would definitely warrant digging deep into the 'bottom of the box' an expression that means wearing one's most expensive and beautiful attire reserved for special occasions. Such and many other 'who's who' occasions often provide vintage opportunities for a parade of the very best clothing lines ever designed. No one ever attends such and many similar occasions on bikers' jeans or night wear. As a matter of fact, people regularly spend an awful amount of money to purchase special attires for such special occasions as detailed above. I will save the reader from a longer catalogue of wardrobe consciousness and requirements. But one thing is sure, no one can deny the fact that certain occasions require that one adorns special and often expensive wardrobe items.

This then leaves us with two very important questions

namely: Why should such mundane events attract more gorgeous dress codes than when we stand before the King of all kings? Does spirituality abhor exquisite and fashionable dressing as many Christians appear to make it look? It is this author's opinion that the answer is a resounding no; for whereas the world should not necessarily be the model for God's people in matters of dressing, there is something that Christians can learn from all the examples cited above. The world did not create fashion and beauty, God did! All the beautiful things and products of human intelligence cannot, and must not be surrendered to the world community out there. Great inspirations originate from a great God as gifts for the unmitigated enjoyment of his children in the world. Beautiful and fashionable clothing belong in that realm too.

There is clearly sufficient room for dressing up for special occasions and that includes when we go to the house of worship. There must therefore be no single accommodation for dressing haggardly or sloppily to church as is often the case with many. Haggard dressing is by no means a display of piety. Just as it would be tantamount to breaking protocol to stand before the Queen of England in casual attire upon the rarest invitation to the Buckingham palace, so I consider Christian worshipers breaking protocol whenever they are casually and shabbily dressed to church where God invites his children in a great demonstration of fatherly fellowship. When we dress beautifully and come before God, we acknowledge in the first place that God himself is beautiful and benevolent towards us. Our appearance bears testimony to our immense love and respect for God, and that he is so kingly that we simply have to think twice about ways in which we can convey our reverence of him in our appearance. Conversely, when we come carelessly and disrespectfully dressed, we convey a low image of God's majesty. We speak without words that he is a king so lowly in the echelon of kings that we can appear any time before him on biker's jeans and work overalls.

The "bottom box" Concept: The "Bottom box" is a popular hypothetical reference among the generality of Africans for burying one's most gorgeous and beautiful dresses in the lower decks and the safest parts of the box or wardrobe. The 'bottom box' is akin to the Western idea of "Sunday best". This concept originates from the times when people only displayed clothes used on a regular basis while carefully folding away the most expensive and gorgeous ones in boxes mostly reserved for special occasions such as church services, weddings, balls and other high profile social events and invitations.

This concept still runs deep among very many Christians as evidenced by the fact that Sunday mornings are always a beauty to behold as men and women resplendently dressed make their ways to the numerous worship houses. The pews reveal color and beauty of unenviable proportion; such indescribable beauty that is probably only matched by the variegated natural shine of the butterfly. There is in a sense, the idea that dressing in a special way to go before God is reflective of God's special and thoughtful way of relating to us as his children. God is very intentional in his dealings with his children. He does not simply do things. He is mindful of things that will make his children rich without adding sorrow (Proverbs 10:22). When he promises to give life he promises one that is more abundant (John 10:10a), and for those who would dare to call to him he shows great and unsearchable things that are yet inconceivable. (Jeremiah 33:3). This is the kind of God for whom his children must seek to approach and respond to in worship with a mood and an appearance that convey joy and hope. This appearance would always, ideally have to entail reaching deep into the 'bottom box' to ensure that the best selection appropriate for honoring the one who himself reached deep down into his bowels of mercy to select his very best, his only Son as savior of the world.

Fearfully and Wonderfully Made: King David was one of the worshipers who understood all too well, the amazing works of God in the lives of his children. He saw the wonders of God's sense of beauty in himself and was subsequently moved to sing God's praise: "I praise you because I am fearfully and wonderfully made; your works are wonderful, I know that full well." (Psalm 139:14). As such, it would be unthinkable to imagine that he wouldn't be very thoughtful about how he appeared before the God

Worshiping Disorders

who he holds in such highest esteem. There the law of attraction that "like attracts like". Things with the same dispositions are quite often, naturally drawn to each other. In that sense one can safely conclude that beauty begets beauty, and beauty is often attracted to beauty. A beautiful God quite naturally appeals to the beautiful senses both body, soul and spirit, of his children on earth. King David was fully aware of this.

It can be said to an extent that the way in which a person appears before God, spiritually or physically is a function of how esteemed or otherwise God is in the person's eyes and to the person's understanding. My knowledge of those who worshiped carved idols in certain towns or villages for example, is that of skimpily dressed priests and priestesses, looking gaunt and famished and with faces painted with white chalks and often bare-footed as they stoop to enter to their mud walled and roof thatched shrines. Such people make no claim of the class or beauty of their gods and goddesses and therefore have no reason to appear otherwise. Consequently, it would be incongruous to see the followers appear in their "bottom boxes". Conversely, it would be a sorry sight to see people dressed like them appearing before the God of Abraham, Isaac and Jacob. The Christian God is a God with class! He is one spoken about only in superlative terms. Christ will never be degraded and humbled again. The "gentle Jesus meek and mild" is now the reigning champion in heaven and on earth where billions of people worship him daily. The moment he completed his task of saving humanity on earth he was immediately glorified never to be vilified again. The crown of thorns immediately gave way to the crown of glory while the robe of righteousness displaced his captive garment and his torn and stinking grave clothes. He now enjoys an overwhelming and unapologetic glory and indescribable beauty in heaven. Popular Nigerian gospel singer, Steve crown, overwhelmed by Christ's majesty came out with a song hit currently making waves all around the gospel music world in which he said of Jesus, "Everything written about you is great!" Knowing all this, it would be a contradiction in terms therefore, to show up before this God in ways short of intentional worshipful dignity.

Shabby or undignified dressing can never be a sign of piety or humility in relation to going to church as some people often make others to believe. Shabbiness is not the same thing as 'soberness'. 'Soberness' describes reasonability and moderation while shabbiness describes dirt, gloominess, irresponsibility and ignorant spiritual grandstanding! Conversely, I must also acknowledge, the most beautiful clothing is not an indication of upright standing before God either. We only dress well to reflect the goodness and beauty of God himself not ours primarily. Our appearance must carry the message that our God is good and able, even in the face of undeniable life's challenges. Our dressing must convey hope, not the opposite, to those who look up to us as people who worship a joy giving God! There must be something responsible and inviting about us that makes a statement concerning the God with whom we have to do. Those on the outside must be able to look again at us and see the Lord's goodness not just within but also outside Thus giving a careful thought during the course of the week about what to wear to church on "The Day of the Lord" is not only about preparing our inward state but also preparing the outward for a privileged encounter with the King of kings. Doing so shows that there is an intention; a conscious anticipation, a self-awareness of just how majestic, how special the chief host of every Christian gathering is. That chief host is God himself. When this type of awareness drives a person's worship life, there is likely to be quality and meaning in the act itself. Neglecting this often-overlooked aspect of who we are and how we should appear to our meetings with and before God clearly makes it a worshiping disorder of the highest proportions.

Dressing well versus Worldliness: In addressing this important issue of dressing for church, it is important to draw a line between what is generally acceptable and what is indecent. This line is particularly essential especially knowing the degree of challenges the body of Christ faces in the world as we know it today. Nearly everything that separates decent and indecent dressing appears to have been erased in the world we know today. The worldly fashion sense will clap and approve of anything that makes people look exclusive and attractive, which raises the question, attractive and exclusive to who? Obviously, it should matter where people dress up to go to. Many people generally embrace worldliness in their attire often to the admiration of persons of the opposite sex especially when they attend social events. One often hear such words as 'sexy', 'dressed to kill', 'provocative' and 'baring it all' used to describe dressing and hailed in most of those places. As a Christian, would you want your dressing to be described as sexy by people? Do you regard such a description as a compliment or as a warning sign that you are becoming worldly and can cause sin to hatch and mature in the hearts of other believers or even non believers who look at you? What examples are you setting forth for younger people around you and for young Christians who look up to you? Should your fashion icons be people who have no regard for the God you serve?

Even if you liked a particular style and would want to copy that, is it not possible to alter it in such a way that it will still reflect the holiness and sobriety required by your God and respected within the Christian community to which you belong? Do you not care that you can constitute a distraction to other worshipers by your flamboyant dressing and makeup that have no room for sobriety? That worship team member who stands to lead people into the presence of God, do you not care that your dressing may be distracting people instead of making them concentrate as they enter into the worship experience? That usher that welcomes people to church, do you create images through your dressing that colonizes the imagination of some people whom you welcomed to church? Can you really afford to compete for attention with God when you claim to be singing or his majesty? By all means, these are simply just a few questions to get one and every child of God thinking and engaged over the issue of dressing as you select what to wear to church next Sunday.

However, much as it would be inappropriate for anyone to legislate on matters of dressing, this note of caution by Paulsell is worthy of note, "If we are to honor our bodies, it is imperative to pay attention to how adornment frees or constrains us. What is constraining for one person can be freeing for another"[33] Everything that we do as members of the community of God should be done in moderation! (Philippians 4:5) I will also like us to heed the warning that no one should constitute a stumbling block to another member of this community. (Romans 14:13). Therefore, mutual care and careful consideration for the sensibilities of one another is a significant aspect of what it means to be true worshipers.

Hygiene and Offensive Odors

A careful look at nature also shows that God created different plants and flowers that give off sweet fragrant scents. That should give us an idea that God likes to perceive good and not bad odors. In the Old Testament worship, the use of incense was very prominent. In several passages of scripture God talks about 'sweet smelling savors', 'perfumeries and spices'

---

[33] Paulsell, p.67

that played a prominent role in the beautification of the body, the temple and its surroundings. A good example that comes to mind is during the beauty parade in which the young Hebrew girl Esther was selected as queen. It was recorded that the young women were set apart and their bodies treated with many different scented perfumes in order to prepare them for the selection process for the next queen. (Esther 2). Esther excelled over several other potential queens to emerge as the chosen one, thanks to the perfumeries and spices generously lavished on her with great care. Also, a look at the New Testament reveals that scents and perfumery were variously admired and embraced. For example, Mary Magdalene endeared herself to Christ by pouring an expensive jar of scented oil on him. While Judas Iscariot felt bemused at such a "waste" of precious resources, Jesus thought otherwise and promptly corrected him. At Jesus' death also, different scented oils were used to anoint his body. Today in the Catholic and Orthodox traditions, burning of incense remains a common practice not only for any spiritual invocations, but mostly for the issuance of sweet smelling aromas in and around the church. In addition, Saint Paul uses the metaphor of 'fragrance' or 'aroma' to describe the lives of Christians. He writes, "Our lives are a Christ-like fragrance rising up to God. But this fragrance is perceived differently by those who are being saved and by those who are perishing" (1Corinthians 2:15, NLT). By no means would Paul have employed such a strong metaphor if

Worshiping Disorders

he ever perceived that God was averse to sweet fragrances. It would seem very unnatural therefore, for any right thinking person to prefer foul odor to a pleasant one. The sensory environment within the church should and must always be the concern of everyone. It is common knowledge among very many people that a foul scent turns people off and pushes some away not least inside the enclosure of the church. This obviously is nothing to be too spiritual or too defensive about.

This brings us to the question as to how some Christians come up with the notion that using scented soaps, creams, powders and perfumes are against the worship of the most High God. This category of people may significantly neglect personal hygiene. Some Christian worshipers come to the sanctuary looking disheveled, unkempt and throwing out some stench that often put those sitting around them in a difficult state as they struggle to hold their nostrils in controlled breaths. In the extreme cases, some people who are unable to withstand the not so pleasant odors find ways of politely moving away to other pews. This not only creates confusion and unwarranted movements but can also be a serious source of embarrassment for the persons concerned. To illustrate this, I will mention the problems my church encounters once in a while. Our church is located next to a PUB and Night Club. Many times some patrons of the club straggle into our meetings, attracted by our heavy but irresistible joyous African beats. If you imagined that they never smelt nice then you would have guessed right. In most cases their alcoholic stench is simply very off-putting to say the least. For the period they stay with us we always feel like God was leading us into temptation in view of the biblical mandate to let people come just as they are.

This issue of personal hygiene is very critical because it can be a problem for many even outside church. It can be a source of conflict between spouses when one party fails to take the issue of hygiene seriously against all expectations and promptings of the other. Unwashed mouths, unwashed bodies, unwashed hair, unshaved armpits, dirty stockings and other underwear, smelly shoes and boots, unlaundered clothes and jackets etc, are all capable of throwing very disturbing stench throughout the immediate vicinity of where the guilty person is sitting.

The sanctuary of worship must be lighted up with the sweetness that will compliment the genial and joyous atmosphere that often prevail in the house of worship. No one should be made to put up with foul smell in whatever situations and circumstances. It is an act of great incivility for untidy worshipers to disregard the sensibilities of other brethren. These untidy persons invade the personal space of others.

However, we must sound a note of caution here. In putting on perfumes and sprays, people should consider other worshipers in terms of the intensity of spray. One person's sweet smelling perfumes may in fact be another person's poison or source of discomfort. Also, some people may have allergic challenges to certain categories of perfumes. Since it is not possible to know the various challenges that people have with regard to difference fragrances, it would therefore make sense to encourage everyone to be moderate in their application of body perfumes. However, where the problems posed to certain members of the community are disclosed, either as a result of allergies or medical conditions, an appeal may go out to the entire church to completely abstain from perfumes for the period of the service for the wellbeing of others. Where such is the case, church leadership must then take proper steps to ensure a minimally acceptable scented atmosphere conducive for everyone.

"Dressing" the Worship Environment (Litters All Around)

The physical atmosphere of the worship space must be seen to be as important as every other consideration in our discussion of worshiping disorders. The vast majority of people cares about their surroundings but would not care about the sanctuary of worship. Most readers would recognize the popular saying that, "Cleanliness is next to godliness". No person wants to sit down for a couple of hours in an uncomfortable environment. Old and dilapidated toilets and bathrooms are capable of polluting the atmosphere within the entire church building. The discomforting pungent smells coupled with their untidy looks would clearly not bring anyone close to godliness if the above expression is anything to go by. Most visitors to a church understand the high value placed in domestic hygiene in their own homes. When a church therefore fails to ensure that facilities within the church property are properly maintained on a regular basis, they expose participants to undue feelings of discomfort, which in turn are capable of keeping certain some of them away from future participation. In addition, a polluted and unattended worship facility stands the risk of posing health hazard for worship participants, something which is completely unexpected in a house where decent devotees, constantly gather on a regular basis.

Church administrators must endeavor to take the necessary steps to ensure a clean and decent environment conducive to both worshipers and visitors to the church. The power of sensory and visual perception on a person's ability to relax and carry out tasks cannot be underestimated. Efforts must be made to ensure not only environmental cleanliness but also, moderate and affordable interior beautification of the sanctuary. People coming to worship the Lord in the beauty of his holiness must be able to do so under a minimally beautiful and clean environment.

Related to this point is the need to ensure that people pick after them when they or their children mess things up in and around the church premises. It is a disturbing act of indiscipline when a person litters the church with used cups and other disposables like used diapers. Yes, some parents leave their children's used diapers in the toilet trash cans! This act must be deemed a pure act of indiscipline, a lack of consideration and respect for God and other worshipers which must be repudiated and stopped at all costs. Most parents would not leave used diapers in their kitchen or toilet trash cans at home because their homes will surely be filled with unpleasant odors, so why do they do so in the house where the Almighty God is worshiped? This is equally true of parents who are in the habit of indulging their children with food, cookies and candies during the service. It is common knowledge that children are very likely to spill liquid all around the church floors when they run uncontrollably around during the service. Church pews and surfaces are pelted with bits and pieces of these 'chewables' and gums stuck into children's mouths by parents who seek to pacify them with just about anything.

It is important for all who are concerned; adults, parents or toddlers' care givers should pick and clean up after them. Failure to do so runs counter to the collective need to keep the house of God in a clean shape. But also, it creates additional work for church officials most of whom are likely to be unpaid volunteers. Such church volunteers can be pushed into grumbling when fellow worshipers create avoidable tasks for them, causing them to spend additional hours cleaning up other people's mess. Unfortunately, those who offend the most are often hesitant to join in doing the tasks that they create for others. It would be wise to heed Dr. Dale A. Robbins warning in an article he titled, "What People Ask About Church":

> "The Lord never intended for the whole ministry of the church to be carried solely by the pastor or a mere handful of people. It's sad that the majority of the work is done by the same faithful few, and sadly, this has caused the "burnout" of its many outstanding workers. If everyone would simply pitch in and do their fair share in helping, serving, giving, and so forth, all the needs would be met and no one would be overburdened."[34]

Worship and care for God's house is a collective calling that ought not to be left for a few. Whatever we do to ensure the health of our house of worship is in itself an act of worship to the Lord, even before we say a word. That is where it all begins!

---

[34] Dr. Dale A. Robbins *"What People Ask About Church"*

BEER-PARLOR ATTITUDES AND CANAL INDULGENCES

Beer-Parlor Attitude:

The beer parlor is a space that very many people know all too well either through patronage, association or simply through awareness of things that go on in the society around them. The image that a beer parlor evokes is that of a place for casual evening or weekend relaxation; a place where casualness replaces serious mental engagement or conversation. The atmosphere is usually as informal and ordinary as it can possibly be. The sight is usually one in which the patrons comfortably sink back into couches and tables with cigar trays, and with beer mugs and most often, engage in casual talks, gossips, jestings and jokes. Indeed the beer parlor to all intents and purposes, provides its patrons with a platform where every encumbrance of life is, ideally, temporarily suspended inside the dark chambers of alcohol and in many cases, of highly intoxicating substances that often don't provoke productive reasoning. Thus as one would expect, the environment is typically arranged to cater for several unrushed hours of unproductive socialization under the highest levels of unchained feelings of comfort and fun, or so the patrons think!

But those are beer-parlor settings and, as expected, a giraffe is expected to have a long neck. Almost no one is under any illusion that gatherings in such meeting spaces will be any different. There is however, a fundamental problem whenever the atmosphere in a worshiping environment is wittingly or otherwise reduced to the casual levels witnessed in a beer-parlor setting. Many may wonder whether there are possibilities that this can indeed occur in places of worship. A careful appraisal of some of the occurrences in church may clearly betray such attitudes even if no one takes such behaviors to heart. Where such occur, the atmosphere created and witnessed by serious-minded participants is one of a bunch of unprepared and unserious folks offering what can be best described as look-alike worship.

Nearly every religion in the world fully recognizes the inherent message embedded in the body language of worshipers. Bodies' postures speak and in many cases they speak the loudest. They communicate willful surrender or obtuse or concealed disagreeability or disloyalty. Through it, an unwilling worshiper is revealed and forced obeisance is detected. It is akin to a reluctant pupil forcefully dragged into the classroom. Such a pupil never sits relaxed. Both the legs and the entire body are all the time positioned away from the centre of attention and no one is under any illusion that such a student is present in the class. I recall those days of my childhood, when my parents would wake me up in the early hours of the morning for family morning devotions. My body language did not only betray a sign or feeling that a child had been treated unfairly, perhaps literally abused by a forced prayer call, but it also constituted a discouragement and unwarranted distraction to all others present. The first line of a protest is often via the body language. Even in important business and diplomatic negotiations, people often observe the body language as an unwritten code of agreement or disagreement. Some people may wonder why body posturing should necessarily be such an issue during worship. Is it not our spirit that is primarily involved in the worship act after all? Is over relaxation necessarily an indication of disrespect or disinterestedness in the business of worship? These are very pertinent questions worthy of our candid consideration. Perhaps, we can begin by acknowledging the fact that nearly every religion, except perhaps the Christian religion is very strict about physical movements and physical gesticulations during worship. It would be unthinkable for participants in many of those religions to sit down when it is the time to bow their heads or when there is a command to fall on their knees. Within these religions, body obedience is as important as spiritual surrender. Yoga practitioners would not sit when the command is to stand, neither would they stand when it is time to sit with legs folded across each other and with hands clasped. The bottom line is that in some other religious there are no personally contrived ways of positioning one's body and selective participation in the worship rituals. Everything is done in tandem with the commands of the worship leader. In such environments, there can be no talk of relaxation akin to what obtains in our description of beer parlor atmosphere.

Yet many Christian denominations contend with those worship participants who view church as an extension of their living rooms. It is for this reason that I guess that almost no church traditionally fills its church hall with easy rocking chairs, although this is a shifting trend lately especially within the ranks of some wealthy mega churches around the world. I have personally been a guest to a church where the pastor's corner was arranged in the mold of a typical cozy mini parlor sadly, with a rocking swivel chair and a tea corner neatly and invitingly tucked in for the drinking comfort of the said pastor. As if that was a mere joke, I was shocked to see the pastor actually being served tea or coffee while the rest of the people were deeply engaged in worship with songs and music. Only one person was not participating - the pastor of the church. This to me was a classical example of an attitude that ought not to be in the worship sanctuary, not least from persons who ought to know better. The truth is that wherever provisions are made for too much comfort on the pews or on the altar, church authorities unwittingly aid and abet 'beer-parlor' attitudes in church. Alertness and mobility are of the essence in any worship session and worshipers ought to always keep that in mind when they decide how to position themselves. In an article published in the Antiochian Orthodox Christian journal, Fr. David Barr addresses this issue succinctly. For example, he points out the issue of leg crossing, which, obviously he considers one of the indicatives of the beer-parlor posturing. Drawing a comparison between attitudes in some Orthodox churches and the churches in North America he writes:

> In some Orthodox cultures, crossing one's legs is taboo and considered to be very disrespectful. In our North American culture, while there are no real taboos concerning crossing one's legs, we tend to cross our legs to get comfortable while sitting. Should we cross our legs in church? No. Not because it is "wrong" to ever cross legs, but rather because it is too casual - and too relaxed - for being in church. Just think about it, when you get settled in your favorite chair at home, you lean back, cross your legs, and then your mind can wander anywhere it wants to.[35]

Understandably, leg crossing is obviously a habit most likely to have been long formed by the people that do it. As such, to them, it would not be considered as a disrespectful way of sitting in the church. Sometimes it can be the preferred sitting position for some especially whenever they want to achieve concentration. Consequently, it seems that in approaching this type of highly controversial issue, we need to put the weight of the argument beyond

---

[35] Fr. David Barr "Church Etiquette or Some Things You Should Know While in Church"

ourselves and our personal comfort or preferences. We do not leave our houses to go to church for our own sake, neither do we go primarily for the benefit of our own convenience. We go to church to worship our creator, the King of all kings who has called us to a life of sacrifice having shown us by his example how to sacrifice personal comfort for the sake of others. Jesus had no such privilege of comfort and relaxation. Here is what Jesus said of himself when a Jewish teacher offered to follow him at a time when he wanted to take a tactical retreat from the crowd, "And Jesus said to him, "Foxes have holes, and birds of the air have nests, but the Son of Man has nowhere to lay his head." (Matthew 8:20). Jesus was always on his toes and going about his father's business, most times under very hostile conditions. Like Jesus, nearly every apostle ministered under very unfriendly and harsh conditions without the type of comfort which easy and feel-good Christianity has made possible in our day.

There are more reasons why a beer-parlor attitude must be condemned and rebuked in the sanctuary of worship. One of such reasons is that it might be disturbing and distracting to other participants. Let us for example, look at the scenario where a Christian lady is dressed in loose or tight and short clothes. If she sits with her legs crossed, there is the tendency that her dress will fall to one side if it is loose, or ride up if it is tight, thereby exposing her thighs and inner garments. What could be more distracting than when someone is ministering and looking down on or struggling to hold gaze away from the indecent exposure. In a case like this, persons with such potentials to expose themselves and who reject advice to change their dressing and comportment shouldn't be allowed to sit in locations that would make it possible for them to distract others.

In addition, our positioning warns our body about how we feel. For example, sitting in a slouching position tells the body that it is time to let down your guards and sleep. On the contrary standing up or sitting upright when we feel sleepy tells the body to wake up and pay attention! When I was a young Christian, our all night prayer vigils were regarded as training times so we held them in the open fields. One of the reasons for choosing such locations was to prevent people from slouching on the chairs and dozing off. If one attempted to sit on the grass, it would be wet because of the dew that had fallen on it. As a result, one was encouraged to stand up and move around all through since sitting will cause wet clothes and buttocks. This way, the body maintained the alertness needed for the long night of prayer. That discipline has remained with me to this day and I still mostly maintain a standing position when praying! From the above, it does seem that not only does the physical posturing of our bodies have implications for what it means to be respectful of God but also, on our ability to maximize concentration.

God's people are under a holy obligation to behave appropriately and respectfully in worship. This is because no other spiritual activity provides Christians with the opportunity to demonstrate the giftedness of the body as conveyors of respect and loyalty to God more than worship gatherings. Through worship services, Christians are handed the rarest chance to recognize the greatness and majesty of God. In some sense, this recognition is not to be seen entirely as a condition of the heart and mind but also, and expectedly so, as behavioral patterns designed to show the highest levels of respect to God. A lack of observable reverent attitude may promote self in worship rather than God. It is an attitude that waits to refuse commands and show utter disregard for other worshipers. Those who display this type of attitude very often betray an attitude of disrespect and pride where they should show the opposite.

For example, we can look at how worshipers behave during the Holy Communion service. It does appear that much of the church is fast losing the traditional solemnity and awe with which this segment of the worship services has long been associated. In our present time, many people approach the Lord's Table with disrespect and unseriousness. It is not uncommon to see some communicants on their way to the holy Table conversing and laughing, and in some cases playing and joking with each other in manners that diminish the power and significance of the act. They pay little or no attention to the performance of the communion liturgy thereby already excluding themselves from the worshipful aspect of the event. Others go towards the table chewing gums or candies and displaying a clear lack of concentration and interest by staring all the way through at any and everyone along their path. There is little sign of enthusiasm or anticipation as they approach the Table, and it is as if they really are not sure of the meaning of the act in which they are involved. This is especially true among young communicants who do not yet seem to fully grasp the true significance of the Table to the body of Christ.

Bishop George V. Murry, S.J., narrated his experience concerning this attitude towards the Eucharist while he visited some of his parishes:

> "When I visit parishes on weekends, I often see parishioners chewing gum in church and even coming to Holy Communion chewing gum. At one parish, a woman came to Communion wearing a sweater that said "World's Sexiest Grandmother." At another, I watched a teenager who was sitting with her parents text throughout the Mass. One priest told me of a man who came to Communion while speaking on his cell phone. When I have spoken to some of these people after Mass and asked them about their behaviour, I usually have gotten the same response. "I'm sorry; I forgot I was in

church."[36]

This clearly represents the attitude of many, and such can only take place wherever people come to church with a mentality of irresponsibility and a lack of seriousness. In such cases church gets mistaken for just about any club or play house down the street.

Also, often during such segments as singing and congregational prayers, it has become common in our day to observe some worshipers sit back nonchalantly on their seats with legs crossed or hands in pocket in ways and manners more befitting of a beer parlor setting or a movie theater for that matter, than of a sanctuary of worship. Yet some others display a flagrant act of disobedience by refraining from liturgical commands such as calls to sit, stand or kneel at various segments of the services, even though there are clearly no physical challenges preventing compliance to such calls. In private as well as in corporate worship such attitudes as these persist, thus putting a big question mark on such persons' true understanding of the majesty of the one they have come to worship and the need to be civil to and respectful of the worship leader and other participants.

As I pointed out in a previous chapter, these kinds of posturing are never manifested when we address

---

[36] Bishop George V. Murry, S.J., "Bad Manners at Church"

people that we consider significant within the society. Such people often command complete attention with gesticulations that smack of reverential regard. Whether it was before powerful bosses or an adorable bride, life often brings people to such situations where they stand in awe of someone that holds much meaning and significance to them. Unfortunately our attitudes towards God in worship largely lack such levels of courtesy and reverence. We often pray, sing and worship in manners that make one to wonder whether indeed the one who is the subject of our worship is simply of our kind and perhaps one who does not deserve much honor.

Christian worshipers must however understand that they share this same world with cultures and societies where people are so respectful of the god of their different religions and perform some bodily rituals to demonstrate that regard. In some religions all worshipers must take off their shoes and wash some parts of their bodies as a matter of compulsion while yet some others never even wear shoes at all while in the worship space. As for the women, theologies aside, many consider it a voluntary, unforced act of reverence to cover their hair before entering the sanctuary. They view such behavior partly as a sign of personal condescension and humility, or simply an act of obedience to their own contrived interpretations of biblical injunctions on the subject. In some extreme cases, some women even go as far as covering their entire faces all in a bid to show some reverence to God or their gods. I am not about to enter into

Worshiping Disorders

theological arguments concerning the polemics of hair covering or other forms of outward show of reverence with all their attached controversies. Nonetheless, such controversies are no replacements for personally ways of showing deep and total reverence to the Almighty God.

In the days of God's people Israel, it would have been taken for granted that God's own people would hold him to the highest honor and esteem. Unfortunately, that was evidently far from the truth. We know because God brought charges against them and complained that he received the greater honor from "people of other nations from morning till night." (Malachi 1:11a) than his adopted children were ready to offer him. Earlier in vs.6 of the same chapter, Israel was also confronted with a very worrisome question. "The LORD of Heaven's Armies says to the priests: "A son honors his father, and a servant respects his master. If I am your father and master, where are the honor and respect I deserve? You have shown contempt for my name!" (Malachi 1:6 NLT)

We must notice here that the priests were the accused in this verse, which appeared like questioning to what degree the ordinary Israelite were prepared to hold God in honor if the priests failed to show the way. Quite unmistakably, God demands the highest form of honor for himself and rightly so, and whenever he fails to receive the same from his children serious reprimand from him followed. However, it must be pointed out that this reprimand is not a demonstration of frustration on God's side. Rather, it is a sign of God's insistent and continuing love and desire for an unbroken fellowship with the children he loves and has given so much to.

To sum up this section, I would say that approaching the altar of God's presence with a lack of decorum and observable disrespectful posturing must be regarded as classical worshiping disorder. In many societies, courtesies and other codes of respect for seniors and other people of significance are easily recognizable. Such persons are never approached with a beer-parlor attitude. Instead they are honored and must be made to see that they are honored, even if deep inside, such honor is only theatrical. Sometimes even more seriously than spoken words, certain patterns of comportment displayed when a person approaches worship can betray a lack of readiness or desire to acknowledge and revere the God before whom the person stands. While it would be extremely difficult however, to come to an agreement as to what attitudes may or may not qualify as discourteous due to the definition of courtesy in different societies, there is not a single doubt that some of the attitudes that make it to this list might sound at least a warning bell whenever we stand before God the Almighty.

Worshiping Disorders

Ministry of the Stomach

Worship is not a very easy exercise. That is why both Jesus and many Bible authors placed a lot of emphasis on that subject. Worship is real hard work, and every worship liturgy is a compendium of series of activities that take time and concerted effort. Consequently, worship requires a level of sacrifice if it is to be focused entirely on God. A significant part of this sacrifice rests in the ability to disregard anything that moves attention away from God to the worshiper instead. This is where the issue of personal canal indulgences comes into this book as a worshiping disorder. This is probably one of the big topics that hardly make it to most Christian literature. However, it is no less one of the factors of disruption in Christian worship.

Very many people find it hard to sacrifice the very least during the worship of the very same God who sacrificed no less than his only begotten son. Many worshipers act as if they have discovered a novel definition for the concept of "total worship", a concept in which spirit, soul and body must be engaged simultaneously during worship. Consequently, while the former is deployed in upward adoration of God, the body receives its own through a constant ingestion of one thing or the other. Sights of worship participants eating candies, cookies, drinking takeaway coffees, or occasional sips from soda mineral bottles even when it is absolutely unnecessary, and the like are very common in many churches. There are also instances of worshipers taking cigarette breaks and subsequently retuning to rejoin the service, naturally with tobacco-smelling mouths that make concentration difficult for their non-smoking neighbors. Indeed every believer ought to understand that when people gather in worship, the food that God wants to feed them with is not necessary Manna and Quail. Rather the food he wants to give them is that of his Holy Word and faith.

This sacrificial element which is associated with the worship hour of God's people has largely come under enemy attack. Hebrews 15:13 speaks of offering to God the "Sacrifice of praise". Sacrifice entails the willful surrendering of some comforts and conveniences. There can be no talk of sacrifice when a person appears not to have sufficient reason to dedicate the time allotted to worship exclusively to God instead of the belly and the taste buds. To see such behaviors is not such a big surprise though. One can expect that to happen among persons for whom worship has moved from a privileged sacred invitation to mere weekly routines. In addition, when contriteness and spirituality are lacking in a person's life, one can always anticipate selfish conducts such as this. But there may in fact be more to this kind of behavior than meets the eyes. In other words, it may actually also be indicative of a more serious development in a Christian's life. In many cases where such behavior is manifest, a personal reverence and fear of God coupled with a sense of decorum and biblical self-control may in fact be a concealed symptom. In that case, a personal contrition and self-discipline is required urgently.

Some folks might however, argue that we need to feel relaxed before our God. To such people, Steve Pruitt has a word of caution. In his article titled "Worship and Reverence" he observes,

"We should always approach God with seriousness and respect. I understand that (God) is our father, and we are invited to crawl up in his laps for hugs and kisses. But we must also understand that he is almighty God and honor and glory are due his name"[37] Truly, God wants us as close to him as possible. But on no account must we view such a privilege and loving condescension as an occasion to be disrespectful and self-satisfying. Clearly, to bring our ever-insatiable canal cravings to some form of subjection at least while worship lasts is a clear lesson on self-denial on our part. Part of what we can glean from our common sense and biblical teaching as well is that there is a time for everything under the sun (Ecclesiastes 3). Many churches offer refreshments after worship services and this is quite commendable Perhaps, this provision will help to contain the ministry of the stomach when people realize that opportunities exist for refreshment and for catching up after the service.

---

[37] Steve Pruitt, "Worship and Reverence"

Worshiping Disorders

It is expected of true worshipers to dedicate the entire duration of the service as a fasting sacrifice to God. There shouldn't be such concept as an 'Eating worship service except of course the Eucharist which is Christ's own invitation to his Table. In every worship event, the greater glory and reverence of God must always be paramount. The ultimate purpose of every worship hour is to cause God to enjoy while we dedicate ourselves as the instruments to make his enjoyment happen and happen in the best ways possible. When we have made God to enjoy, he abundantly satisfies all our own heart's longings. A popular Igbo proverb says that no one ever goes to the house of a king and returns home empty handed. Wouldn't that be truer with regards to being the source of pleasure for the King of all kings inside his own sanctuary? I will conclude this chapter by quoting the prophet Habakkuk who writes, "But the LORD is in His holy temple. Let all the earth keep silence before Him." (Habakkuk 2:20).

Worshiping Disorders

WAITING IT OUT

In the fifth chapter, we addressed the endemic problem of late attendance to church services. In this chapter, I will address yet one other practice that is equally of worrisome proportions. There are people who have cultivated the habit of leaving church before the formal dismissal without seeing anything wrong with it. The Benediction is generally the common marker of the end of Christian worship meetings in many parts of the world. The *Benediction* (Latin, *Benedicere,* translated as *the Blessing* in English, is not just the technical way of concluding a church service, it is one of the most anticipated moments in the service as evidenced in the ways and manners in which participants take seriously the blessings that are pronounced by the worship leader. Many participants at a worship service view this pronouncement as the last dance, the dance that will launch them into a long week of hope and joy, enough to sustain them until the next Sunday. One wonders then why anyone would want to miss this very vital segment of the service by walking away in the middle of it. The general understanding and feelers from people who try to explain this phenomenon usually boils down to the issue of time.

Discussions surrounding has become increasingly problematic in Christian worship and it is very easy to understand why. Many people subscribe to the popular maxim that 'time is money'. The church exists

Worshiping Disorders

in a world where time has increasingly become a non negotiable property.. In this kind of world all sorts of steps are taken to ensure that there are quick and instant fixes for virtually every sphere of human activity. Science and technology are daily finding solutions for time consuming human activities in order to ensure that all valuable time is profitably converted to cash or other pleasurable and profitable endeavors. For example, there is a near complete eradication of the once time consuming home cooked meals in exchange for fast foods, especially, but not exclusively, in the west. In other words, family kitchens have for the most part been relocated to the street corners. In Sweden there are places referred to as "Gatukök" literarily meaning "Street kitchen". They are all over the place offering a wide range of delicacies and they often well patronized by every class of society.

Aside from the proliferation of eat-as-you-go chains, there is also the prevalence of 'Instant Foods' which has apparently come to fill in whatever little space families have to be able to spend time together in the kitchen space of their homes. It is evident that nearly every grocery store without exception has enlarged its instant foods departments to accommodate the increasing vulnerability of families that appear to have been liberated from burdensome and time consuming traditional cooking methods. From instant noodles, packed salads, packed pasta, frozen pizza all the way to instant coffees etc, all that matter is anything that will get people going without taking much of their time. Garrick Saito (2013) rightly observes that "Eating out provides the path of least resistance". He goes on to list the following as some of the reasons that justify the habit of eating out or doing quick-fix menus, "Planning a meal takes time; Shopping takes time; Food preparation takes time; Serving takes time; Washing dirty dishes takes time"[38]

Real concern for time challenges people's ability to nourish their bodies with well cooked and nutritionally balanced homemade meals. With this kind of trend in the society, it is no surprise that fast food attitudes are fast gripping people's ability to settle down and worship without much emphasis on the time factor.

This is precisely the case! It is all about time. Apparently, this enemy appears to have found several victims inside the church. If not, why would a person walk into a worship service already mindful of time? There is a sense that many people have this attitude of giving God a time limit outside of which they would withdraw their precious worship. God seems to have become a buddy who gets time notification from his patrons, for since when did Christian worship become something to be compared to a stand-up entertainment show? When did commitment to the worship of our great God adopt such an austere attitude with respect to time? Of course, one fully understands the general reasoning of

---

[38] Garrick Saito

many people concerning the need for proper time management during worship, something which I am fully in support of. The problem is that irrespective of whatever time constraints that individuals may have with regard to time, the worship of God ought to not in any way be reduced to a spiritual fast food restaurant where people walk in and out at will. To my mind to walk out of a service before it ends literary amounts to quitting God's presence prematurely. This is without prejudice for those who on occasion would have genuine reasons to leave especially where dismissal time is exceeded due to some circumstances or miscalculations by worship leaders. Such reasons may range from Sunday work shifts, health concerns, family emergencies etc. Aside from such helpless circumstances or emergencies, no reason should be deemed reasonable enough to quit service before the Benediction.

Perhaps, if there is any reason to justify unnecessary premature exits, it would be for the same reasons that church is the only place where people suddenly wake up to things that would never matter to them under other situations. For example, the same person who will be very relaxed to watch a block buster movie for nearly three hours without complaint will exhibit signs of impatience with a service that is lasting for one and half hours. Or is it that a Harry Porter movie is more interesting or more deserving of a person's time than a church service, even if the movie starts later or ends later than expected? Also, the same persons who go to watch their favourite sports icons play, whether at the stadium or at O'Leary's, games that often last no less than 90 minutes excluding injury times and sometimes extra times of added 30 whole minutes in the case of must-win matches, is not willing to concentrate in church in the rare cases of delayed closure of 10 minutes. Similarly, when people attend parties and social events, one never gets any sense that anyone present cares anything about what the clock is saying. Church is the one unfortunate handy culprit of people's complaints when once their perceived comfort is infringed upon even in the most minimal way. It makes no sense at all that the Christian's spiritual hospital, the Christian's spiritual restaurant, the Christian's family house and conference hall where the chief host is God is the only place worshipers are so eager to leave at the earliest opportunity.

D.H. Utah, reflecting over this issue of time spent in church makes a very emotional case citing the fate of Christians who experience deprivation in terms of opportunities to worship. He observes, "Who are we to complain about the length of services when many, many Orthodox around the world have suffered greatly, some laying down their very lives to 'get through' church."[39] I see a huge and unfortunate paradox here. Those who have unfettered access to worship protest being kept for too long in church while those who would want to be nowhere else but church are denied the opportunity to go there due to

---

[39] D.H. Utah

intense persecution. The question then is, is it better to be persecuted or to be free? Of course Bible history shows that at such times as ours when personal convenience begins to supersede the pleasure and purposes of God, he was always quick to bring about an affliction and scattering that brought his people back to their senses. We know all too well that each time there is a natural disaster in our current dispensation nearly everyone affected quickly rediscovered the house of God and many actually remained there for a few days and perhaps weeks, until help arrived.

Time to Start and Time to End

When should a church service start? How long should it last? When should it end? These are valid questions that many readers will be eager to have addressed especially in view of the issues discussed in the preceding section. Also, is time management a valid concern in worship services? Should there be rigidly set times to start and end a service? As a matter of principle there should and there ought to be! God himself is a God of discipline. He is not an 'anything goes' personality. However, one must be extremely cautious in approaching a subject such as this simply because the movement of God's Spirit cannot and has never been reduced to strict human conventions, irrespective of human concerns about time. Most often, the mathematical equations of God defies $1+1=2$ because his sense of mathematics is not the

Worshiping Disorders

same as ours. This is the same sense in which the Apostle Peter warns saying, "But do not forget this one thing, dear friends: With the Lord a day is like a thousand years, and a thousand years are like a day." (2Peter 3:8)

Now, does this negate the earlier assertion that God is a God of discipline? Not at all! How then must we make sense of this? We can make sense of it when we understand that God has no particular obligation to us with regards to time, necessarily. When it comes to the matter of time really, it is we that always have to yield not him. Does that mean the church should not designate starting and closing times for services? It does not mean that at all. Churches must do well to make such provisions. However, they should also keep in mind what makes the church different from other organizations that conduct conferences and seminars. It is a Spiritual body where the Spirit of God can sometimes overrule man's timing. Sometimes, even secular seminars and conferences exceed designated times as some participants can get carried away by well presented arguments. Whenever such happens, participants may not walk out on the speakers and planners neither does anyone visibly display a feeling of anger and dissatisfaction as worshipers often do toward their pastors and other leaders. These are facts most readers know all too well. The church as a living organism better stands in a position to occasionally place an extra demand on our time when the need arises, and whenever such is the case we ought to very gladly oblige. Robotic

Worshiping Disorders

mechanisms can never apply to spiritual engagements because spirits are not robots. Thus, worship loses its living soul once it loses its inherent freedom to create unanticipated contingencies. This fact was demonstrated in Acts of the Apostles 20:7-11, earlier referred to. Paul's speech lasted well into the night, apparently well beyond scheduled closing time and one of the participants fell asleep, consequently falling headlong from the window and died. This unusual incident opens the opportunity for one of the greatest miracles credited to Apostle Paul who acted fast in faith and prayer to quickly bring the dead man back to life! We were not told that any of the brethren walked out on Paul in protest for poor time management that may have caused a tragedy. Rather, these people who lived in an agrarian economy and who probably needed to wake up early to go to the farms to graze their animals simply rejoiced at the miracle that unfolded before their very eyes. They understood the importance of Paul's message at the time and they were prepared to wait it out and they had had the opportunity to see for themselves how the power of God could be at work even to the raising of the dead. That happened because the participants surrendered completely to the unchallenged flow of God's spirit.

Let's look at it this way; if theatre goers, people attending music concerts of their favourite artists, circus and carnival attendees and the like, can sometimes get so carried away that the screams of "more! more!" would feel the air, why would such

Worshiping Disorders

moments be repudiated when on occasion they happen during a spirit-filled worship service? Why are Christians so terribly impatient and intolerant of some rare moments of divine visitation whose manifestation is usually beyond the prior knowledge of anyone? Where are God's people actually rushing to? Why do they always attempt to accommodate God within the confines of the tiny cubicle of their own sense of time? There is an old popular saying that "The patient dog eats the fattest bone". Of a truth, only the patient can receive anything from God. Only the patient waits long enough to watch the stirring of the pool of God's benevolence. The spirit of God has a way of overruling human plans when he chooses to. This is part of what it means to say that God is sovereign. "The wind blows wherever it pleases. You hear its sound, but you cannot tell where it comes from or where it is going." (John 3:8). Jesus made the above statement when he was dialoguing with Nicodemus, a learned Pharisee man who was attempting to lecture him on the natural course of biology. He was very correct. A man simply cannot enter into his mother's stomach to be born a second time. But again, in purely spiritual matters, the laws of science and natural order atrophy. Jesus goes ahead with a lesson on what happens when the wind, (Hebrew 'Ruach') blows. When that happens, it blows wherever it pleases without anyone having ability to determine its origin or direction. The point here is this; even though every possible human effort must be made to ensure proper time management during every worship service everyone involved in directing the service and the participants alike must be sensitive enough to know those rare moments when it would be spiritually suicidal to stop a particular act of grace or visitation by the spirit of God. What needs to be clearly understood also is that such moments may not always fall within our 'two-hour' service framework or whatever time allotted by each church, else we would assume that we can pin God's spirit down to our own limited concept of time.

It would work best for us to understand that we cannot under any spiritual legal grounds force the spirit to always bend to our rigidly designated time frames. Because God is sovereign, he may choose to visit a sinner a minute before the end of service; he may visit another with a convincing word of prophecy; he may begin a healing process in a person's body in ways that baffle one and all and he may choose to do any of those at such a time that deflates everyone's expectations regarding patterned management of time. Whenever such is the case, it would be very selfish for people not to tarry a little longer in solidarity with the spirit and with the benefactors. Cooperation with the spirit in times like these however, would be seen as a high level recognition that although we own our precious time, God owns both us and our time. Sometimes rushing out or better put, walking out, may not mean we will get home early. Those who reverently and sacrificially walk with God quite often cover more mileages than those who start earlier but filled with their own understanding and rigidly set in their own ways. An African proverb has this to say; 'Where those who are running will get to; those who are walking will get there too.'

A Continuing Struggle

With all said, I will add that I am not trying to excuse tardiness on the part of worship leaders and ministers. Worship participants should understand that many ministers admit that they struggle with time management. However, it is more serious with some than it is with others and sometimes it affects some more than they are willing to admit. Perhaps an objective admission I would love to make here to assuage the feelings of readers who may be tempted to accuse of me of being an advocate of disorderliness is that the philosophy of "As the spirit leads" as a justification for overshooting service times must be deployed sparingly. It is only the spirit that must determine when and how he leads and whenever he leads a service to close later than slated, he will always bear witness in many present at the meeting that it is indeed he who is keeping them a little longer. Usually once that happens, many participants would be calm and accommodating of the extra time. However, it should become a matter of concern if late closures become a regular pattern something for which many of us including this author stand in need of God's help to overcome. On the other hand however, worship leaders should also be sensitive to those other times when the spirit will lead them to close the service earlier than the usual time. The spirit could also decide that the visitation had happened within a shorter time than originally planned. The spirit does not always lead towards one direction!

A final word! What should be your attitude as a worship participant when your pastor or worship director struggles consistently with late service closures? Should you walk out on them or continue to show tolerance? Walking out on anybody is a gross uncivil behaviour. It shouldn't be encouraged under any circumstance, not least on the person you call and respect as your spiritual mentor. We all have weaknesses or challenges in some areas of our lives. How would we feel if people walked out on us instead of offering some help or advice? This of course, as pointed out earlier, is with the exception of persons who have very genuine reasons to leave service such as work or matters of exceptional importance that cannot wait until the formal end of the service. Secondly, walking out on a worship service would amount to an irreverent act towards God himself. Remember that whenever you walk through the doors into the sanctuary, you cease to be primarily responsible to anyone but God who is the reason for your coming in the first place. It does therefore matter what you do and how you behave while still within his courts. In addition to all the above, Fr. David Barr observes, "Leaving church before the Dismissal -

besides being rude - deprives us of a blessing".[40]

There is indeed something akin to rudeness and disrespect whenever you walk out on a church service unduly. Always keep in mind that your pastor or worship leader is also a sinner saved by grace through faith like you. Keep in mind also, that just like you, they are still works in progress. You may wish to find this particular area of their lives a weak spot that should constitute a prayer point on their behalf. Most people often do not see the need to pray for their pastors and worship directors and all they do is stand by and criticize. If you therefore find this weakness then pray and seek the attention of those who really can communicate the general concerns to them if you can't communicate it to them. It is God that changes people not mere unhealthy human criticism and gossip both of which should have no place among God's people.

---

[40] Fr David Barr.

Worshiping Disorders

CONCLUSION

Perhaps, a significant part of the problem experienced in Christian worship stems from the fact that immediately upon becoming a Christian, a person is suddenly confronted with a barrage of unfamiliar patterns of behavior, whole new ways of doing things that were previously alien to the person. Adjusting to life in a new kingdom often involves confronting the unfamiliar which includes learning to live under the king of that kingdom. Quite often, the subjects of a powerful king don't insist on their own patterns of conduct. Their own ways and preferences are surrendered to the pleasure of the king. Christians are through Christ adopted into the kingdom of the King of all kings, thus necessitating a complete switch to the patterns of behavior in the kingdom of this King. Whoever thought such would be very easy! The apostle Paul aptly describes this sudden shift in status in his letter to the Ephesians Chapter 2:12-13 thus, "…that at that time you were without Christ, being aliens from the commonwealth of Israel and strangers from the covenants of promise, having no hope and without God in the world. But now in Christ Jesus you who once were far off have been brought near by the blood of Christ."

A former sinner who becomes a member of the family of God faces the challenges to adapt to the codes of conduct in the new household. Christians were once strangers to the 'commonwealth of Israel' and aliens to the divine ways of doing things. Prior to adoption into God's family, no one could truly take pride in having any ideas of how to behave in his presence. Thus getting it right with worship is never a guaranteed conduct of any and everyone. This can be likened to what happens when a commoner is married into a royal family. Adjustments in behavior to reflect the public's expectations of royal conduct usually become a huge challenge. Christians need to realize that they enjoy a royalty of far greater prestige than any earthly royal family enjoys. Consequently, far greater demands are placed on them to be prudent in the ways they behave especially when they are within the precincts of God's holy court, but definitely not limited to it, since our entire bodies constitute God's temple and we live and move and have our beings in him, (Acts 17:28). Apostle Peter also calls Christians "a chosen people, a royal priesthood, a holy nation…" [1Peter 2:9].

Author Christensen again echoes this royal privilege of ours when he observes: "We are part of the divine family which is not just an assembly of people. It is a community in Christ"[41]. Our chief royal court or palace is the house of God. Once there, we must be able to recognize who we are; that because of this God-given status, we are no longer allowed to behave in some ways, especially in ways that 'dumb' down our new status and reduce the power of our devotion to our God. Once conscious of that, we are then able to

---

[41] Christensen, p.23.

Worshiping Disorders

appreciate our own obligation to behave in ways that are both pleasing to the one who has called us, as well as sync with the new status that we have graciously assumed. Only then can we have a high and unforced sense of reverence and awe, stripped of all worshiping disorders. We should be so consumed with gratitude that all we would want is to get lost in the worship of this Holy One. Only then can we truly serve the Lord with "fear and trembling" [Psalm 1:11], and learn to say like David "But as for me, I will come into your house in the multitude of your mercy: and in your fear will I worship toward your holy temple." [Psalm 5:7, AKJV].

Worshiping Disorders

GOING FORWARD

A focused and determined effort at a worship renewal can play a huge role in eliminating much of the worshiping disorders that we have variously examined in the preceding pages. Robert E. Webber has written so much about the need for worship renewal, which is not necessarily the primary focus of this essay. However, some of the sentiments that he expressed in his book "Worship Is A Verb" tend to resonate with the main concerns of this book. People would behave better and find more meaning in worship if what goes on in it holds some substance for them. In other words, when a worship service is both engaging and filled with the presence of God, participants are most likely to pay more attention thereby, desisting from many of the negative points raised here.

As I reviewed some of the worshiping disorders, I was able to for instance, locate why I never took Sunday evening services very seriously during my years in my local church in my native country of Nigeria. A sense of dryness pervaded the entire duration of the service of those years, so much so that one literally needed some form of stealth activity to hold back sleep or boredom. Some of those activities came in the form of playing with just about anything or cat-talking with friends sitting close by and on occasion, loitering around waiting for the end of the service. Unfortunately, such service had the tendencies to last for eternity. Webber observes that "One of the problems of evangelical worship is the passive nature of the congregation" who do nothing else than "just sit…and sing a hymn or two and put money in the plate."[42] The result of this becomes even clearer from Christensen's remark that "Many people whether they admit or not…attend (worship) more as spectators of a performance rather than as participants in the worship of God."[43] This has always been and still remains one of the major culprits to negative attitudes in many churches. One sees no reason for flippancy and passivity in an atmosphere of worship where people walk into the sanctuary sensing the presence of God right from the entrance to the sanctuary and ultimately drawn in as active participants instead of passive observers. The saying that 'an idle mind is the devil's workshop' obviously seems to hold some truth in this circumstance.

It remains very surprising that many churches in the West for example, still run what I may call a "one man show" during their services. By that I mean that the priest leads the music, leads the praying and also responds with the usual monotonic 'amens' while the congregation look on in misplaced holy silence. In many of these congregations the people say nothing at all except to sing and pray our Lord's Prayer and then sing the Nunc Dimitis and make their ways home. It must be said that such outdated styles of doing worship finds no much place at all in this

---

[42] Webber, p.12.
[43] Christensen, p.13.

increasingly noisy world, not least when young people are part of the service. On this same issue Christensen has this to add, "Passivity for the worshipper is no longer valid today. Communication and growth is accomplished through interchange of thought and dialogical involvement"[44] Every church where the opposite is the case risks leaving important segments of the worshiping community behind. This probably accounts for an increasing shift in church allegiances that sees the younger generation drifting to the new generation churches that speak to their world in terms of worship style and engagement, leaving the main line and orthodox churches struggling to maintain the 'ancient landmark'.

There is immense power in the sound of many voices and the hearts most often get activated by the resounding echo of the voices of the people. The moment people begin to truly encounter God in their worship with hearts and voices raised in unison and unity, they will inevitably give up most of, if not all irreverent behavioral patterns that arise from worship services that do not take the person of the Holy Spirit seriously. Whenever people make the rules and regulate worship, lethargy and incapacity often follow. On the contrary, wherever the Holy Spirit is present in power, freeing people to enter into the Holy of Holies without any human-made bottlenecks, there is scarcely any room at all for any manifestation of ill or unwholesome behaviors that constitute worshiping

---

[44] Christenson, p.24

Worshiping Disorders

disorders. Worship and fellowship are the highest and the most pleasurable out of this worldly experience that God gave to humans. When both are directed at him and fellow believers, his presence empowers people to be able to overcome all obstacles.

This quote culled from the Ministry Magazine aptly summarizes the very heart of this book, and pushes back the task of restoring the right etiquette to the worship of God. It observes,

> The Supreme Being is worthy of highest reverence; therefore we must discover how to bring profound reverence into the worship of the Almighty in the churches under our guidance. God gave rules of order, perfect and exact, to priests and people long ago, for their conduct in the ancient tabernacle. God's ways have not changed. We must correct the disrespect, all too prevalent, that has dishonored God in His sanctuary."[45]

When church leaders assume their positions in this wise, they will lead the way for God's people to follow, and the Lord God will be worshiped in the most reverential ways possible. God's people will also treat one another with great respect and civility.

---

[45] The Ministry Magazine

REFERENCES

Barr, David. Fr, "Church Etiquette or Some Things You Should Know While in Church", http://www.antiochian.org/christianeducation/etiquette. (Retrieved on July 10, 2017)

Bishop George V. Murry, S.J., "Bad Manners at Church" Friday, 13 May 2011,

http://doyorg.ipage.com/files/index.php?option=com_content&view=article&id=479:bad-manners-at-church&catid=37:bishops-column&Itemid=54, (Retrieved on August 6, 2017)

Christensen, L. James. *Don't Waste your Time in Worship*. Fleming H. Revell Company, Old Tappan, New Jersey, 1978, pp.13,19

Cornell, Steve, "What does Postmordernism mean?" October 24, 2006.https://www.summit.org/resources/articles/what-does-postmodern-mean/ (Retrieved on August 11, 2017)

Davies, J. G., *Every Day God*, SCM Press Ltd, London, UK, 1973, p. 268.

Dawn, J. Marva. *Reaching Out Without Dumbing Down*. William B. Eerdmans Publishing Company, Grand Rapids, Michigan1995, pp. 27, 97, 259, 267

DeBonville, John, "Stop dressing so tacky for church" CNN blog, April 19th, 2014 http://religion.blogs.cnn.com/2014/04/19/stop-dressing-so-tacky-for-church/, (Retrieved on September 22, 2017)

Dobson, James *The New Dare to Discipline,* Illinois, Tyndale Momentum; Reissue edition: 2018.

Elochukwu, E. Uzukwu, *Worship As Body Language*, The Liturgical Press, Collegeville, Minnesota, 1997, pp.15, 19.

Forerunner, "Proper Sabbath-Service Behavior", May 2000, http://www.sabbath.org/index.cfm/fuseaction/Library.sr/CT/RA/k/94/Proper-Sabbath-Service-Behavior.htm (Retrieved on July 3, 2017)

Herbert, A. S. *Worship in Ancient Israel.* John Knox Press, Richmond, Virginia, 1959, p.5

Horn E. H. *Worship in Crisis.* Fortress Press, Philadelphia 1972, p.3,

Leonard, R.C. "A Sensible Approach to Christian Truth", Laudemont Ministries, http://www.laudemont.org/a-wjcsaw.htm (Retrieved on August 7, 2017)

MedlinePlus, US National Library of Medicine, https://medlineplus.gov/ency/article/000341.h

(Retrieved on September 6, 2017)

Omenka Egwuatu Nwa-Ikenga, "Honoring your Ancestors, Odinani: The Sacred Arts &Sciences of the Igbo People", January 26, 2011 (Retrieved on February 2018)

Padfield, David, "Sleeping Saints", The church of Christ in Zion, Illinois) http://www.padfield.com/1995/sleep.html, (Retrieved on September 7, 2016)

Paulsell, Stephanie. *Honoring The Body, Meditations on a Christian Practice.* Jossy-Bass, John Wiley & Sons, San Francisco, CA. 2002, pp.60, 67.

Pritchard, Ray, "Risky Business: The other side of freedom" Keep Believing Ministries http://www.keepbelieving.com/sermon/2001-08-12-Risky-Business-The-Other-Side-of-Christian-Freedom/ (Retrieved on September 20, 2017)

Pruitt, Steve, "Worship and Reverence", http://justworship.com/holy-reverence/#more-1360, (Retrieved on March 4, 2016).

Robbins Dale A., "What People Ask About Church", http://www.victorious.org/cbook/chur41-help-church (Retrieved on September 12, 2017)

Rodríguez, Am.M. " The Ark of the Covenant", Biblical Research Institute, https://adventistbiblicalresearch.org/materials/theology-sanctuary/ark-covenant (Retrieved on September 4, 2017)

Rowley, H. H., *Worship in Ancient Israel; Its Forms and Meaning*, Fortress Press, Philadelphia, 1967, p.257, 257

Saito, Garrick "What are the major reasons why people don't cook at home more often?", https://www.quora.com/What-are-the-major-reasons-why-people-dont-cook-at-home-more-often, Amateur weekend cook. Avid Food Network watcher. Updated Aug 14, 2013). Retrieved on October 14, 2017.

The Canadian Mar Thoma Church Toronto Sunday School Newsletter "Be on time" http://www.canadianmarthomachurch.com/userfiles/file/Sunday%20school%202017%20-2018/Jan-Mar2017-Newsletter.pdf (Retrieved on August 9, 2017)

The danger of Lateness to church, http://naijasky.com/christianity/1756/the-danger-of-lateness-to-church/8127/ (Retrieved on May 2, 2016)

Truett, Cathy S, "It's Better to Build Boys Than Mend Men" (Book title), Looking Glass Books,

Georgia, 2004.

The Ministry Magazine, "Reverence in the Church Service" https://www.ministrymagazine.org/archive/1940/10/reverence-in-the-church-service Retrieved on October 16, 2017

Webber, E. Robert. *Worship Is a Verb*. Word Books Publisher, Waco, Texas, 1985, pp.16, 107

"What does the Bible say about being late or lateness?" https://www.gotquestions.org/late-lateness.html (Retrieved on November 2, 2016.)

Zavada, Jack. "What is Postmodernism? Discover Why Postmodernism Conflicts With Christianity." https://www.thoughtco.com/what-is-postmodernism-700692 (Updated June 17, 2016 and retrieved on September 9, 2017)

Worshiping Disorders

ENDORSEMENTS

Dr. Samuel is a true pioneer in the arena of religious studies. In his new masterpiece *Worshiping Disorders*, Dr. Nweze, demystifies the heart of true worship by showing the world the hindrances to a pure heart of worship toward God. As a leading global voice in faith based leadership, Dr. Nweze's voice always adds to the equation of excellence among people of Faith. This book will bring the reader into a new perspective of self learning and a closer walk with their Creator. I highly recommend every faith based institution to make this book a priority in their curriculum. The heart of a matter must be looked at clearly in order to produce the results needed for a better life and to provide better service to others. Dr. Samuel E. Nweze, is one of the true genius minds in the world today. He is making the world a better place. This book will go down in history as a great work of art.

Sir Clyde Rivers, World Civility Leader & Founder IChange Nations

In reading his book *Worshiping Disorders,* it's clear to me that Reverend Sam knows his audience. Little did I know, that audience was me! His candid insight to our lackadaisical approach to worshiping the One who gave us life, breath, and being in the first place, is a necessary corrective to our current worship practices. A first step to *"Worshiping Well"* is to spend some time reading this book and reflecting on the ways we're personally and corporately cheating ourselves and others when it comes to our encounter with God in worship.

Rev. Douglas Fondell, pastor of the American Church in Paris.

Worshiping Disorders is an expressive masterpiece, a clarion call to reverential discipline during Christian corporate worship. This is, no doubt, a didactic prototype and invaluable resource material on good Christian etiquette and discipline. This knowledge-based Christian narrative is devoid of ambiguity of meaning, scriptural blemish and misinterpretation. All sincere worshipers who desire to experience God's manifest presence on a regular basis will find this book very helpful. Samuel Nweze, as a well-known Christian music minister and devout worshiper, drawing from his wealth of experience, presents his ten- chapter book in a clear, instructive and prescriptive manner. I have no hesitation, therefore in recommending this work to all and sundry, especially to all visionary Christian leaders and Heaven-bound Ministers of the WORD.

Bishop Ransom Stephen, J.P, Ch.MC; President, Association of African Pentecostal Bishops and Chaplains (AFRIBAC), Nigerian Hqtrs.

In an excellent way the author has sensitised Christians to behaviours that are ungodly yet have permeated the very fibre of our Christian life. He brilliantly captures with completeness, the major reasons and theories that influence our reverence of God our maker. He also suggests great improvements that I think should be preached in all churches. I recommend this book to every Christian who truly wants to take the heavenly race very seriously to attain the crown that awaits us there.

Joe Etbon, Council Chairman, The Uniting Church in Sweden, Hallunda Parish.

Dr Sam Nweze has poured out his heart in this well-presented text, drawing from his long experience as a Worship Leader in his native home in Nigeria and internationally. It is a heart-cry to ministers and the laity to return and worship the Father in Spirit, in truth and in humility of heart that marks the redeemed of the Lord.

Dr Richard E Nnabuko, Christ Redemption Church, Enugu, Nigeria

At a time when people are resorting to a plethora of religions, cults, and unpopular belief systems; the legendary Rev. Samuel Nweze documents the rarely talked about worship disorders. It is a great book written from the heart for uncertain times for seeking believers. Read this book and use it as SatNav to navigate the spiritual disorders as you search for the Infinite. Read and transcend your popular religiosity. Read and develop your spiritual ability to have a heart-to-heart encounter with God.

Worshiping Disorders

Professor Patrick Businge, Chancellor of Greatness University London

ABOUT THE AUTHOR

Samuel E. Nweze is the founder and pastor of the International Congregation of the Uniting Church in Sweden, Hallunda parish. He is an experienced and passionate Intercontinental worship leader, teacher and counselor. He has recorded albums with various artists and groups. He also has a personal audio album titled *Nothing Impossible* to his credit. He is the founder of the popular pandemic lockdown-birthed online gospel music Talk Show *GSTN Sweden Live* (Gospel Songs Then & Now), which he co-hosts with his wife Ebere.

He holds a Master of Divinity degree from North Park Theological Seminary Chicago, Illinois and a Bachelor's degree in English studies from the University of Ife, Nigeria. Samuel also holds an Honorary Doctorate degree in Christian leadership. He is a World Civility Ambassador and an inductee into the World Book of Greatness. He lives in Stockholm, Sweden with his wife and four children.

Worshiping Disorders

www.ingramcontent.com/pod-product-compliance
Lightning Source LLC
Chambersburg PA
CBHW071159160426
43196CB00011B/2130